Suffering With Purpose

To Cindy —

My dear High School friend —

Nancy
6/17/2016

II

Suffering With Purpose

A scriptural guide for anyone who is hurting

Larry M. Arrowood
Woodsong Publishing
Seymour, IN

Suffering With Purpose: a scriptural guide for anyone who is hurting
Larry M. Arrowood

2013

This is a revision of Surviving The Storm of Suffering, originally printed in 1995 by Prince of Peace Publishers
Woodsong Publishing
7100 Persimmon Lake Drive
Seymour, IN 47274

Most Scripture quotations are from the King James Version of the Bible unless otherwise identified. Some quotations are from The Message. Copyright © 1993, 1994, 1995, 1996, 2000, 2001, 2002. Used by permission of NavPress Publishing Group

All rights reserved. This publication may not be reproduced, stored in an electronic system, or transmitted in any form or by any means, electronic, mechanical, photocopy, recording, or otherwise, without proper credit to the author. Brief quotations may be used without permission.

ISBN 978-0-9649570-9-1

Printed in United States of America.

Table of Contents

Dedication
Chapter 1 — The Season of Suffering
Chapter 2 — Survival Manual
Chapter 3 — Profile of Suffering
Chapter 4 — The Certainty of Suffering
Chapter 5 — The Questions of Suffering
Chapter 6 — Response to Suffering
Chapter 7 — The Response of Friends
Chapter 8 — God's Response
Chapter 9 — Helping Those Who Suffer
Chapter 10 — The Reward of Suffering
Chapter 11 — When Suffering Doesn't Make Sense
Chapter 12 — Daily Trust
Chapter 13 — When the Pain Won't Stop
Chapter 14 — What I Have Learned
Chapter 15 — Finding Your Rainbow
Chapter 16 — Christ's Suffering

Dedication

This book is dedicated to the host of parishioners with whom I have associated during forty years of ministry, who suffered much, but their suffering never destroyed their faith and commitment to Jesus Christ.

Chapter 1

The Season of Suffering

> For what glory is it, if, when ye be buffeted for your faults, ye shall take it patiently? but if, when ye do well, and suffer for it, ye take it patiently, this is acceptable with God. For even hereunto were ye called: because Christ also suffered for us, leaving us an example, that ye should follow his steps.
>
> I Peter 2:20-21 KJV

It was early morning of our final day in a Great Smoky Mountain cabin. We celebrated Valentine's Day a few days prior and reflected upon our many blessings. I had spent the week writing and relaxing. Nancy, my wife of forty-one years, had enjoyed shopping during the day and lounging evenings with a book. We were ready for home, refreshed, and excited about life.

I awoke early and enjoyed some final moments before the packing began. Nancy hadn't stirred, and I hated to wake her. When she awoke, her sudden and strange movements alarmed me. Without speaking she methodically slapped her cheek. "What's going on?" I asked. Her guttural response surprised me. For the first time in our marriage, we couldn't communicate. I watched in utter disbelief, wondering why she awkwardly smacked her cheek with her left hand. I didn't want to accept the obvious: a stroke. With the right side of her body completely paralyzed, she thought she was dreaming, and she was attempting to wake herself. She tried, through slurred speech, to respond to my questions. Seemingly helpless, I did the one thing I could; I called 911.

Looking back at that frightful morning we see some humor in the most devastating day we'd encountered. Still lying in bed, hearing the sirens in the distance, she gestured for me to get her dressed for the trip to the hospital. As I had focused on her immediate needs, I'd failed to clothe myself. I had to make a decision. Do I dress her or myself? No way was I going to be caught by the paramedics in my boxers. I dressed myself, and, thankfully, had time to dress her before the ambulance arrived. Our image was spared.

Three years have passed since that terrifying morning. Since then we've see many physicians, tried a plethora of medications, offered much prayer, and have lived on a roller coaster ride of uncertainty. Nancy recovered completely from the stroke only to nosedive into a condition more debilitating than the stroke: leaky gut syndrome. Though the verdict is still out among physicians regarding leaky gut as being a medically established diagnosis, for Nancy it was very real and stole a year of her life. This week we're back in the mountains, and I'm reworking this manuscript that was first published seventeen years ago. I realize now how very little I truly understood suffering back then. Still, no matter how much one knows about or experiences suffering, it doesn't diminish the sting of present pain.

One of the most significant lessons we've had to accept on our personal journey of suffering is no one receives immunity. Not the good or the bad. Not the weak or the strong. Not the poor or the wealthy. Not the sinner or the saint. Not the vilest criminal or the most innocent child. Further, we recognize that anguish and joy are fellow passengers on life's journey. We're still learning to balance our suffering with God's blessing, still learning to offer praise in the midst of pain. Our joy mustn't be snuffed out because of the calamity. We're recognizing suffering and blessing run parallel, like a set of train tracks, and the destination is determined by staying the course. We've recognized on our journey, no matter how turbulent the storm, the Savior remains our traveling companion. We reluctantly identify with the apostle's cry, "That I may know him, and the power of his resurrection, and the fellowship of his sufferings, being made conformable unto his death" (Philippians 3:10).

Suffering With Purpose

Inspired of the Holy Spirit and the wisdom of experience, the Old Testament writer penned the memorable words, "To every thing there is a season, and a time to every purpose under the heaven" (Ecclesiastes 3:1). Birth. Death. War. Peace. Suffering. The cycle has continued since creation's transgression. No matter how hard one tries, no one can stop the inevitable. All will enter into a time of suffering.

I've heard it explained by some, "Life is like the changing seasons." Probably no one has clarified this concept any more succinctly than the world-renown inspirational speaker and author, the memorable Jim Rohn.[1] In this analogy, each year the seasons come, do their thing, and give way to the next. Likewise, life has its seasons. In evaluating this similarity of the changing of life and the changing of the seasons, spring, with birth and newness of life, represents the beginning of the cycle. Springtime opens a door of opportunity and renewed purpose. Whether it's a flower garden or a new endeavor, springtime is the time to plan, to cultivate, and to plant. It's the time of birth: of ideas, of a new business, of a relationship.

Then comes summer, a time to protect and nurture the crops we've planted in the spring. If we do well, and stay on top of the weeds, we'll reap the benefits with fall's abundant harvest.

Spring, summer, and fall represent the good times of life. They're full of challenge and replete with reward. Then comes winter. The season of harshness follows the good times. In the winter we don't produce; rather, we endure. Winter represents hardships: personal suffering, setbacks, social hurts, divorce, failures, economic disaster, disease, and ultimately death. No matter how well we plan we can't stop the impending and changing seasons, and we certainly can't prevent the howling, frigid winds of winter. But even winter has its positive purpose.

I was barely out of college when a colleague explained how everyone must enter into a time of suffering. It's that time of life that makes you or breaks you. Somewhere along life's journey, either early on, at midway, or toward the end, each will experience severe adversity that tries men's souls. It's the predictability of life. No one is exempt. He explained his hardships came early in life, and he was glad to have that part of life behind him. He shared his battle scars with satisfaction, expressing he'd be the better man for them. At the have everything going well for him. I hoped to ...asure of his success. We've kept in touch these many ...ow realize he was only partially right in his philosophy ...uffering. All will eventually experience severe hardship, ...rocess is never concluded this side of eternity. Suffering ...one-time deal where you pay your dues and get a pass for the rest of life. There is no club to which you retire from suffering. Contrary to his philosophy (which he has drastically adjusted since those many years ago), the stories of his suffering in the beginning couldn't compare to what happened to him during midlife. It seemed so unfair and unnecessary. I watched with disbelief as his world crumbled around him, and I saw suffering like I had never seen before. We've both entered into the downside of life, and we stay in touch. I've listened and watched as his latter years have brought him disappointment we couldn't imagine those many years ago when he mentored me about the stage of suffering being isolated to a particular phase in life. I've also noticed he's learned through the years to stay on track, rejoicing over the good things of life and accepting the bad running alongside the good.

I wish my colleague's philosophy was correct, that winter only comes once in a lifetime. If so, I would have experienced mine long ago and have it behind me. To the contrary, we have multiple winters in a lifetime. Sometimes winter follows winter. Encouraging though, God is the God of all seasons, including winter. Winter is not a season out of God's control; rather, it is a season of transition, of enduring, of necessity. Jesus said, "Verily, verily, I say unto you, Except a corn of wheat fall into the ground and die, it abideth alone: but if it die, it bringeth forth much fruit" (John 12:24). God doesn't abandon us during our winters of life; He comes alongside us, and He fellowships with us in ways not experienced apart from suffering.

Four words of John's gospel called to me from the pages of Scripture, " ... and it was winter" (John 10:22). For Christ, this time of His life was more than a seasonal change; it was the beginning of a long and harsh winter in, not only His life, but in the lives of a multitude of His family and friends. He had experienced three years of successful ministry within the Jewish community, so much so that wicked religious leaders, who feared their control over the masses was being eroded, were bent on destroying, if not His life,

Suffering With Purpose

at least His credibility. The ruling Sadducees and pious Pharisees accused Him of not only breaking the Old Testament law, but of blasphemy, a complete irreverence for the God and the teachings of the Old Testament. They tried to discredit His supernatural birth by pointing out His ordinary background and family. "Is not this the carpenter, the son of Mary, the brother of James, and Joses, and of Juda, and Simon? and are not his sisters here with us? And they were offended at him" (Mark 6:3). As an ultimate attack on His character they called Him a Samaritan possessed of a devil. On one occasion He narrowly escaped their stoning. Finally, they convinced one of His associates to betray Him, false witnesses to testify against Him, and the Roman government to consider Him a threat to Caesar. This resulted in His crucifixion.

His followers were devastated; their hopes and dreams of the Kingdom of God among them were shattered. How could this be? Many whom His touch healed and His voice freed were living proof of His miraculous ministry, but now Messiah was dead. They were without hope and confused. They didn't understand how this could happen. Why would God allow it to happen? Though Jesus had spoke of his resurrection, they didn't understand. Nor did they understand no matter how severe the winter, spring always follows. Such is the design of our loving Creator.

Jesus' cry from the cross, "It is finished," wasn't a concession of defeat; it was a proclamation of spring. He announced, "My winter is over; spring is here at last." With His dying breath He declared victory, for Jesus designed spring to follow winter.

After his friends lovingly placed His lifeless body in that lonely and cold tomb of death, the wind suddenly shifted. The season transitioned. The flowers of spring broke forth from the chilly grip of wintertime. Three days later He resurrected. Fifty days later spring broke forth upon His disciples as the warm winds of Pentecost breathed upon them (Acts 2:1-4).

The use of the seasons to explain life's transitions may not hold true in all climates, but the analogy is true among all peoples and cultures. We each enter the winters of life; it's inevitable. The winter takes on many forms, but the symptoms are often the same: fear, loneliness, misunderstanding, pain, sorrow, and death. The motivation for this book is the hope that you will find faith to believe in God's springtime of life and to endure the hardship of your winter. My goal is to encourage you to hang in there until you witness the spring. I remind you we must endure the winter to savor the spring. God's hand is in each of the seasons. Each season can serve a meaningful purpose, though we often cannot see such. God refuses to abandon us, often turning our despair into devotion.

The format of this book is to highlight the wisdom and directives offered in the Old Testament Book of Job, along with testimonials of lives who have endured much hardship but found strength and purpose to endure the winters of their lives. I'm going to share the testimony of some who entered into severe extremes of winter and came forth victorious. We'll discuss the manner in which they learned to wait upon the warmth of spring to bring life back into their souls. We'll see how sorrow stretched their faith to the point of breaking. We'll hear their moans, "I'm finished." Still, they found hope and reason to go on.

As our primary source, we'll survey the Book of Job for some answers to enduring the winters of life. This book uses Job's story as a guide to help us survive the storms of suffering, and more so, to help us find purpose in our suffering. "But Job was a unique man whom God planned all along to bless, and Job made it through his suffering, and God gave him back more than he lost," you say. "I'm no Job." As we study Job's life, there are a number of questions that will remain, but there is one lesson we can learn: Job was just as human as any of us, and his suffering offers us direction on how to endure the suffering of life.

Suffering brings more questions than answers. Is suffering an indication I am out of God's will? I hear testimonies of the victories of others, but why has God not delivered me? Is my suffering of my own doing? Is it punishment for some sin? Why hasn't my deliverance come? Am I a worthless creature even God doesn't care to consider? Mark Batterson, in his inspirational book, The Circle Maker, offers keen insight to this emotional battle.

> "Sometimes when you hear answers to prayer that others have experienced, it can be discouraging instead of encouraging because you wonder why God has answered their prayers but not yours. But let me

remind you that these answers have rarely happened as quickly or easily as they sound. There is usually a backstory. So we are quick to celebrate the answer to prayer, but the answer probably didn't come quickly. I've never met a person who didn't experience some big disappointments on the way to his or her big dream."[2]

Why suffering? This question is quite perplexing. For the Christian seeking a solution from Scripture, the answer can be simplified: it is the call of God. "These things I have spoken unto you, that in me ye might have peace. In the world ye shall have tribulation: but be of good cheer; I have overcome the world" (John 16:33). Paul wrote to the believers at Philippi, "For unto you it is given in the behalf of Christ, not only to believe on him, but also to suffer for his sake" (Philippians 1:29). God may not send suffering to us, but when we suffer, He brings purpose to our suffering. We may never realize the specifics, but God has a unique way of allowing suffering to serve a meaningful purpose in His Kingdom.

It's no coincidence that Paul wrote to the church at Philippi regarding suffering. The account of the founding of their church is recorded in Acts 16. Upon receiving a vision from the Lord, Paul redirected his missionary journey from Asia into the region of Macedonia (northern Greece). With fresh anointing in God's directive, Paul and Silas took the first available ship and sailed on the winds of confidence. "And after he had seen the vision, immediately we endeavoured to go into Macedonia, assuredly gathering that the Lord had called us for to preach the gospel unto them" (Acts 16:10). At Philippi they were thrilled by the conversion of the household of Lydia. Shortly after this victory, a young woman possessed of an evil spirit was delivered. Revival had undoubtedly come to town, but, in a matter of hours, this red-hot revival came to a screeching halt. The evil men who used the young woman's fortune-telling abilities for personal gain became extremely angry. Since she could no longer divine fortunes through the evil spirit, overnight they lost their lucrative source of income. These spiritual pimps stirred up their Gentile customers against these meddling Jews, had Paul and Silas arrested, tried as criminals, and put in jail. In a short time frame, we have the miraculous manifestation of God's power to deliver reversed by evil injustice, and the outcome is a vicious beating and incarceration for Paul and Silas. The Bible expresses they "laid many stripes upon them" (Acts 16:23). A whipping by Gentile authorities could be horribly cruel. In contrast, Jewish laws regarding beatings forbid more than thirty-nine lashes. This was not so in Roman law; it depended upon the judge. From recorded Scripture, there was a lot of emotion evolved in this particular judgment of Paul and Silas, and we can assume the beating was quite inhumane. Interestingly, Paul did not inform them of his Roman citizenship and his legal rights; he does later (Acts 16:37).

Why didn't God intervene on behalf of Paul and Silas to prevent the beating? We can only speculate. God didn't necessarily want them to be beaten and cast into prison, but once the events transpired, God refused to allow such suffering to be wasted. Paul and Silas could have been angry and blamed God for allowing such mistreatment. Instead, they joined with God to allow their suffering to have meaning. At midnight, with beaten and bleeding backs and pain-racked bodies, they sang praises unto God. Suddenly, the miraculous happened: an earthquake shook the prison and the doors burst open. The jailer, who would have been executed had the prisoners escaped, considered suicide, but Paul intervened. Instead of suicide, he and his entire family were baptized into Christ. What a miracle! Ironically, Paul and Silas didn't receive healing for their wounds; rather, the jailer tended to them and washed their open stripes. In his letter to the church at Philippi, perhaps Paul was reminding the Philippian believers how their church was founded: through his suffering. That was the background story. God didn't allow their suffering to happen without giving it purpose. If we must suffer, we dare not waste our purpose in suffering by fighting against the pain, the loss, and the disappointment. We need to live with expectancy that God will bring some good out of our suffering.

By faith we hear the songbirds of spring. They sing a melody of hope. Winter's chill gives way to the thaw of another spring. Though some springs seem late in coming, be patient, for they'll come. The Easter lilies of hope, though lying dormant beneath the soil's frozen crust, have already sensed the signal of spring. Angels stand waiting for a dispatch to either roll away our stone of adversity or else join us in the fight. Either way, Scripture assures victory. In the meantime, to live is to experience the season of suffering.

Points of Discussion

Discuss the concept of happiness and suffering as parallel train tracks. How do we maintain happiness while adjusting to suffering?

What flaws may be present in comparing life to the changing seasons?

How may we prepare to endure the winters of life?

How did Paul and Silas allow their suffering to have purpose? How may we apply this principle?

How may the words of Christ "It is finished" be interpreted from a positive perspective?

Chapter 2

Survival Manual

> Yet if any man suffer as a Christian, let him not be ashamed; but let him glorify God on this behalf.
>
> I Peter 4:16

Sooner or later, suffering strikes each of us and leaves life spinning seemingly out of control. It's at these times we can learn to surrender our lives into the Master's hands. Strength to endure comes through such surrender to Christ and faith in His love. We must learn to trust the promises of the Bible before we experience fulfillment of such promises. Like Job, we learn to affirm, "Though he slay me, yet will I trust in him..." (Job 13:15). Total surrender includes surrendering the past, present, and future. We surrender past victories to apparent defeats. This suppresses hopes and plans for the future. This may resemble defeat, but surrender to God is never defeat; rather, it is assurance of ultimate victory. This is the message from the book of Job. Though Job clung to a golden past, questioned the fairness of the present, and argued his future held no purpose, somewhere during his suffering, he surrendered his will to God.

> Then Job answered the Lord, and said, I know that thou canst do everything and that no thought can be withholden from thee. Who is he that hideth counsel without knowledge? therefore have I uttered that I understood not; things too wonderful for me, which

I knew not. Hear, I beseech thee, and I will speak: I will demand of thee, and declare thou unto me. I have heard of thee by the hearing of the ear: but now mine eye seeth thee. Wherefore I abhor myself, and repent in dust and ashes.

Job 42:1-6

    This manuscript is by no means a commentary on the Book of Job; rather, I've used the story of Job's life to offer guidance through the pitfalls and uncertainties of suffering. For me the Book of Job is a winter survival manual, written out of Job's experience of extreme suffering. I've chosen to focus on his response to suffering as a model for us to follow. Job survived a winter blizzard and lived to flourish in another springtime. Further, his account is recorded from beginning to end: spring, summer, fall, winter. And spring! He leaves a well-documented trail that serves as a roadmap for anyone traversing a trail of tears.

    Job's springtime was exemplary and quite picturesque, as he seemingly did all the right things: extremely dedicated to God, family, and his work. He planned, planted, and cultivated well. Summer found him tending to all that was his, serving God and family, along with providing for a host of servants. The fall of life reaped the benefits: a large and loving family, houses and lands, crops, multiple and plentiful flocks, and a devout relationship with God. Life was grand and the future full of purpose. Then came his winter, when in a single day Job's family and possessions were stripped from him. In a second wintry blast, Job's health was attacked: constant and seemingly unbearable pain. With such unbelievable devastation that befell him, it seemed his winter would last forever, or at least until he passed away from a disease-racked body. The final wintry blast came from the mouth of his only remaining family member: his wife. "Curse God, and die." She had given up, battle weary, emotionally distraught, and spiritually empty.

    His friends felt all was lost as far as his personal possessions were concerned. They set about to rescue his soul: repent or perish seemed to be their message. Job resisted, not their concern, but their assessment of the reason for all the bad things happening to him.

Suffering With Purpose

He defended his reputation of being a good man, so much so that he called God into the picture to vindicate his righteous life.

God's response surprised Job. God didn't seem as pleased with Job's life as Job had assumed. Not pleased with God's response, Job argued his cause with God. When this proved futile, he stonewalled. His stonewalling consisted of verbal silence with lots of gray-cell argumentation. God had the advantage: He could read Job's thoughts. Job finally stopped defending his honor and trying to figure out why all these things had happened to him. Through a painful process he surrendered to God's plan, whatever it might be. Surprisingly, a life seemingly out of control was brought into peace and harmony with its Creator.

To suffer wisely is to surrender our suffering unto Jesus Christ. Oh, but we are tempted to fight back, to challenge, to question, and to complain. However, this does not prevent nor change suffering. Suffering will come to all, lingering longer than we think it should, and with meaningless purpose to those who refuse to surrender their lives into God's care.

The Lord doesn't always reveal nor explain to us the purpose of the multiple battles taking place in the spiritual realm. Job didn't know Satan had targeted him, neither did the Lord tell him. Charles Swindoll, in his excellent biography of Job, observes: "His misery turns to mystery with God's silence. If the words of his so-called friends are hard to hear, the silence of God becomes downright intolerable. Not until the thirty-eighth chapter of the book does God finally break the silence, however long that took."[1]

Such is the case of most suffering: it seems pointless. I've stood in the presence of what seemed inexplicable tragedy and unbearable suffering. During those times, I must confess, I questioned God's reasoning. And, for the most part, after forty years of ministry, I still don't have the answers to many, if not most, of my "why" questions. I've learned there are better questions: "What may I learn through this? How can this help me minister to others? Who may need me to comfort them? Am I becoming more compassionate toward others? How can my life be a positive for others?"

The motivation for this book is not to provide answers to all our questions, but to offer hope to you who are suffering and to help you approach suffering from a meaningful perspective. In order for suffering to be meaningful, we need to, like Job of old, accept suffering as a part of life, to surrender our anger and resistance through prayer, to patiently wait on God's strength to endure the present, and to recognize spring awaits the Christian. Whether this side of eternity or beyond, ultimate victory is Christ's promise!

Points of Discussion

What are typical initial responses to suffering? How did Job's response resemble these? Or did it?

Did the response of Job's wife reflect a lack of spirituality?

What could be a better response to suffering than asking the "why" question? Why?

What are positive ways we may surrender our suffering to Christ?

Chapter 3

Profile of Suffering

> Blessed are they that mourn: for they shall be comforted.
>
> Matthew 5:4

As a pastor, I interact with those suffering almost daily. I am one of the first to be called when tragedy strikes. And though I must confess this revised manuscript still seems inadequate for the magnitude of the subject, if I can help one soul through their hardships I am overjoyed and more than willing to share any insight I may have gleaned from years of pastoral ministry.

Through the years I've witnessed much suffering by family, friends, parishioners, and more recently my wife's chronic suffering. My father, at age fifty-nine, without prior symptoms, was hospitalized with unexplained symptoms. After weeks of tests, a doctor eventually diagnosed him as having vasculitis. At that time it was a rare disease characterized by inflammation of blood vessels and arteries, and it was often fatal. During medical treatment, for unknown reasons, his body reacted violently to the medication, and he lost the majority use of his lungs, a condition from which he never recovered. The outcome was devastating for him: eleven years of chronic pain and total disability from the pulmonary disorder. His health issues never improved; rather, they became increasingly worse: kidney dialysis for years, multiple amputations (ultimately loosing both legs), and many months of hospitalization. Due to frequent bouts of his illness I spent five Christmases in a row at the hospital. Initially, after the shock wore off, we battled anger. Dad originally went into the hospital with a couple sores on his feet; he left the hospital disabled and unable to go back to work. Someone had to be responsible, but we eventually realized blaming didn't reverse the situation. We learned to accept the present conditions and squeeze out of the circumstances any joy we could find. Our large family filled the waiting room for days on end. I'm sure people wondered about such revelry that often took place through those hundreds of hours of waiting. Laughter was the one medication that worked for us, along with lots of prayer. Dad kept a fantastic spirit through it all, but the sickness completely altered his future, as his dreams of retirement shattered, and all so suddenly. Though Dad loved life, because of extreme pain, he welcomed death, but it eluded him for years. Exhausted, we spent the last days with him in a hospice unit. As life had been difficult for Dad, death, too, was a long and painful process. Death brings mixed emotions. For us, it was guilt that surfaced with the relief that a loved one had died.

Suffering has a way of multiplying itself. My wife and I experienced the sickness of my father and both her parents simultaneously. We spent many holidays apart, Nancy at her parents' sick bed and me at Dad's. After multiple bouts of various illnesses, my father-in-law, feeling somewhat exhausted, drove himself to the doctor, which resulted in being sent directly to the hospital. He never returned home. Forty days later we said our last good-byes to him. Nancy's mother survived multiple amputations. We reluctantly placed her in a nursing home. Even though she owned the home, it still seemed cruel to leave her there. She pouted for months. We felt some sense of relief when she accepted life in the nursing home. That's where she died. We have never gotten over the absence of parents. Death was their escape but cruel to the family unit. After twelve years caring for my mother, we've admitted her into a nursing home. The whole ordeal causes a deep ache.

I've fielded many questions regarding suffering. Why did God allow my child to die? Why did the Lord not protect my family? Why do I have to suffer such shame? Why are the guilty allowed to go free? Is there any fairness? Why should the righteous suffer at the hands of the wicked?

It's especially difficult to accept the death of a child. With the passing of years I still see the pain on the parents' faces. I'll mention only one of many. The parents were assured the surgery would be successful, but hours later, all went wrong. For weeks their precious three-year-old clung to life while they clung to hope, but hope did not prevail. I preached the funeral. Many came to offer their support. The nurses who cared for him those many days in the hospital came to comfort, but all they could do was cry. What went wrong? Why didn't God heal him? We still have few if any answers, only questions.

If we should compile a profile of suffering, it would include all the things we shun: hurt, unanswered questions, unfairness, cruelty, loneliness, shock, shattered dreams, unpredictable fears, separation, disease, deformity, pain, and death. Any one of these is enough to send our lives into a tailspin, spiraling us into the depths of despair. Regardless of our response, suffering will continue so long as the earth endures. And it will eventually come to all. There are no exceptions. Too many fight back with anger, depression, self-pity, guilt, withdrawal, denial, and a host of defense mechanisms. But suffering is something we cannot escape. Sooner or later the coiled serpent of suffering strikes. Often it strikes multiple times. Suffering is impossible to prevent. Seldom can we escape its pursuit. We best endure suffering by accepting it, not fighting against it. We must adapt to suffering that co-exists with the happiness God gives.

The process of acceptance is difficult. Acceptance isn't a resignation to inactivity and despair; rather, it is letting go of the "why me" mentality. Each must accept suffering as a part of life that is unavoidable. Sooner or later suffering will knock on everyone's door. No exceptions. This is not to assume a position of fatalism or a sense of powerlessness. We can survive the storm, using the turbulent winds to soar closer to God. How? Attitude matters. Faith makes a difference. We can accept suffering without self-pity. We can reject bitterness. We don't need to blame God. We can view universal suffering as a result of mankind's succumbing to Satan's deception, not God abandoning us. It is the normal state of a fallen creation. It isn't God's punishment; it's what God warned would happen if we lived apart from His original plan. God is not the villain, nor is He obligated to remove the suffering; however, His Word offers instruction regarding suffering.

Christ challenged the false assumption of His day that suffering was a direct result of one's personal sin. "And his disciples asked him, saying, Master, who did sin, this man, or his parents, that he was born blind?" (John 9:2). Christ clarified that suffering isn't necessarily connected with personal sins. "Jesus answered, Neither hath this man sinned, nor his parents: but that the works of God should be made manifest in him" (John 9:3). We are but to look to the Scripture for direction and clarification regarding this false assumption that all suffering is a result of personal sin. Suffering is the plight of mortality. Jesus didn't remove suffering from His own mother. She, along with He, had to endure Calvary. He cared deeply for His mother, and He directed the Apostle John to tend to her needs, but He didn't isolate her from sorrow. Neither did God remove suffering from the purpose of Christ. God cared, but there was more at stake than removing pain from His Son, He was removing sin from humanity. Salvation came at a great cost. If anyone should have been exempt from suffering, it should have been the sinless Christ, who "… was in all points tempted like as we are, yet without sin" (Hebrews 4:15). Christ accepted suffering without doubting God's love. He realized God's love for humanity nailed Him to the cross, and He counted the cost justified. Christ's acceptance of His purpose and means of fulfilling that purpose is our ultimate example for facing suffering. Once we accept suffering, not as God's curse but as the consequence of a long ago decision that plunged mankind into a state of mortality, we are ready to grow, to learn, and to keep on living a meaningful life through suffering rather than merely enduring the suffering.

Our faith, like Job's, will be tested by Satan's age-old challenge that we serve God from a motivation of blessings, and that God is buying our love in exchange for His divine protection from pain. Though some may search for comfortable Christianity, the idea of such is a misnomer. We cannot have Calvary without the cross, Holy Spirit power without prayer, freedom without responsibility, or conquest without battle scars. Neither will we have a life of constant fairy-tale endings; rather, life is peppered with suffering.

> Wherefore let them that suffer according to the will of God commit the keeping of their souls to him in well doing, as unto the faithful Creator. But the God of all grace, who hath called us unto his eternal glory by Christ Jesus, after that ye have suffered a while, make you perfect, stablish, strengthen, settle you.
>
> I Peter 4:19; 5:10

Since the first edition of this manuscript, the list of parishioners whose lives are suddenly turned upside down has grown exponentially. The storms of suffering have blown fiercely in my family. We've lost so many unborn grandbabies it's too painful to spend time reminiscing. We don't know why; it seems useless to ask why. We believe they exist in heaven, and we'll someday see them. Nancy suffered through the stroke, but a host of seemingly unrelated complications followed. The latest was a nine-month stretch of debilitating chronic pain. The doctor said three more months (if she sticks to a stringent regiment). That was eight months ago. Just recently we turned the corner, but the renewed health was short-lived. We're into round two of leaky gut syndrome. I must confess I never thought we'd go through all we've been through the last three years. We are consoled by two things: God's promises of Scripture we've found true through personal experience, and the example shown us by others who have suffered more than we but continue to love and serve Christ with abandon. Many have paved the way; we are but to follow their example.

Later in the book I share the stories of some individuals who have experienced much suffering. Each is tragic and could have left the individuals and their families in utter turmoil. These are the stories of survivors, and by their permission, I share their experiences that you might gain strength and direction. Each account deserves a chapter, so I've reserved them for the end.

Points of Discussion

What are some of your deepest hurts? How did you respond? If you could redo your responses, what would you do differently?

Is suffering a result of personal sin?

How did Christ's temptations allow Him to relate to us?

Discuss how, according to the Apostle Peter (I Peter 4:19; 5:10), suffering can work positively in our lives.

Chapter 4

The Certainty of Suffering

> Yea, and all that will live godly in Christ Jesus shall suffer persecution.
>
> II Timothy 3:12

The sting of suffering is its lack of expectancy. It comes so suddenly. Families leave on vacation with full intentions of returning safely. The surgeon's explanation of the unexpected complications is devastating. The policeman's unannounced visit with the news of a head-on collision rocks any world. Though some know their marriage has problems, they are still stunned when divorce papers are served. We never quite prepare ourselves for the shattering blow delivered by suffering's lack of expectancy, nor can we.

Our preparations for suffering are always inadequate, for how does one properly prepare for suffering? Such was the case of Job. From the Bible land of Uz, Job was rich, famous, and very much at peace with God, family, and neighbors. The Bible describes him as blameless and upright; one who feared God and shunned evil. So noble was he that his concerns were directed away from himself and towards his seven sons and three daughters. However, his concerns were far short of the suffering that befell him that normal day. Concerned his children might have acted in a manner displeasing to God, he offered sacrifices on their behalf. He had no hint that was the last prayer he would pray for them before they met God face to face. He didn't anticipate the curve life was about to throw him.

Nor could he imagine he was God's poster child for righteousness, prompting Satan to challenge God regarding his motives for the righteous life he lived. And it was inconceivable that in a day's time four messengers would arrive with news of such devastation. The first said, "All your oxen and donkeys have been stolen and the attending servants murdered." A second arrived while the first was yet speaking, and through gasps for air he cried, "A fire from the sky raced across the field leaving nothing alive in its path. Your servants and sheep were all consumed." And a third servant brought similar news of the camels and attending servants being destroyed. But then came the knockout punch, "Your sons and daughters are all dead from a tornado."

His crops and livestock were gone, and his present food supply was exhausted. His means of future crops were gone since farming animals and servants were killed. The loss of Job's camels ended his lucrative caravan business. Then came the news from which none could see recovery: the death of all his children. His desire for living probably ended with the report of his family's death. What an awful dilemma and all in a single day!

Let's look on the positive side. Job still had God. Or did he? This is where the mind can become Satan's seedbed. Where could God be in all this? With such tragedy how could he be in God's favor? If these were insufficient to cause him to give up, the test to come would finish him off. At first he says and does the right things: faith talk and worship. As time transpires Job's attitude puts him at odds, not only with his wife and closest friends, but also with God. Sitting upon an ash heap of customary mourning, scraping with broken pottery (an indication of his financial disaster) the oozing sores which covered his body, Job eventually questioned his position with God. He somewhat perceived God as his enemy, for how could anyone cause or allow such suffering to come upon someone they cared about?

If we could receive an advanced warning of approaching disaster, see the impending storm clouds, or hear a warning siren, perhaps we could better prepare for the torrents of suffering. Jesus expressed, "If the goodman of the house had known in what watch the thief would come, he would have watched …"(Matthew 24:43). But this is seldom the case. More often than not, out of a cloudless sky, the storm thunders over the mountains, and as quick as lightning, tragedy strikes. Then and only then, without any emotional preparation, we respond, broken and shaken. With our human, finite minds and fragile emotions, we respond. We struggle and fight back, but the overwhelming odds flatten us. And while down we question, "Where in the world are You, God?" We question our God, our faith, and ourselves. Our world spins. Perhaps this is only a dream, but we awaken daily to reality. We try to go on, but our heart bleeds, draining life. We push on but stumble and fall. Satan, with hands held high in victory, awaits the knockout count. And sometimes we don't have enough energy to even care.

One: Where is God when you need Him?
Two: Why did God allow this to happen?
Three: I must not have pleased Him with my life.
Four: This must be God's punishment upon me.
Five: I can't bear anymore.
Six: How can I go on?
Seven: My God, why have you forsaken me?
Eight: It is finished.

Unlike Christ's proclamation, we are literally saying, "I am finished ... defeated ... wiped out," but somewhere in the countdown, Christ enters the ring. Christ, the despised and rejected One, a man of sorrows, and acquainted with grief! Christ, the wounded and bruised man of suffering! He enters the ring, not necessarily to remove the pain nor sorrow, but to stop Satan's victory count, to speak words of comfort to all who are suffering, "I understand." He gives hope in place of despair. Just as suddenly as suffering comes, Christ, too, comes on the scene. He comes not necessarily with an explanation but with an exclamation, "...I will never leave thee, nor forsake thee" (Hebrews 13:5).

Where is God when we need Him? Ever present! How do we know this? It was a personal promise from Christ, some of His final words to the believers: "I am with you always, even unto the end of the world. Amen" (Matthew 28:20). And though Christ does not always choose to remove suffering, He neutralizes its power with His presence. Though He allows suffering, His presence protects us against Satan's deathblow. The Apostle Paul expressed this condition as being "cast down, but not destroyed" (II Corinthians

4:9). The Phillips translation gives a very vivid illustration: "We may be knocked down, but we are never knocked out."

Satan is not beyond maximizing the pain of suffering. When we are stunned with pain and sorrow, he is at an advantage against our defense. But, as with Job, Satan cannot touch us without arousing God's attention. God limits Satan's power to harm. "And the Lord said unto Satan, behold, all that he hath is in thy power; only upon himself put not forth thine hand" (Job 1:12). "And the Lord said unto Satan, Behold, he is in thine hand: but save his life" (Job 2:6). And to us the Lord has said,

> There hath no temptation taken you but such as is common to man; but God is faithful, who will not suffer you to be tempted above that ye are able; but will with the temptation also make a way to escape, that ye may be able to bear it.
> I Corinthians 10:13

But why doesn't God prevent suffering? I cannot answer this question for God, but I can give some direction from Scripture:

1. God did not bring suffering. Suffering is the result of the fall of man in Genesis. Sin separated man from the ever-present protection of God and the utopia that existed in the Garden of Eden. Man chose to follow Satan's subtle suggestions, even though God fully warned of the consequences. God had given orders regarding expected behavior and the consequences of disobedience.

> And the Lord God commanded the man, saying, Of every tree of the garden thou mayest freely eat: But of the tree of the knowledge of good and evil, thou shalt not eat of it: for of the day that thou eatest thereof, thou shalt surely die.
> Genesis 2:16-17

Even if mankind could reverse his biological blight and become good, his goodness could neither eradicate nor prevent suffering. Diseases would continue. The pain of parting caused by death would not diminish. History has proven mankind is not prone to goodness;

he continues the path away from the God of Genesis. Pastor, scholar, and author Eugene H. Peterson shares in descriptive terms Paul's explanation of the Gentile's downward spiral into debauchery:

> Since they didn't bother to acknowledge God, God quit bothering them and let them run loose. And then all hell broke loose: rampant evil, grabbing and grasping, vicious backstabbing. They made life hell on earth with their envy, wanton killing, bickering, and cheating. Look at them: mean-spirited, venomous, fork-tongued God-bashers. Bullies, swaggerers, insufferable windbags! They keep inventing new ways of wrecking lives. They ditch their parents when they get in the way. Stupid, slimy, cruel, cold-blooded. And it's not as if they don't know better. They know perfectly well they're spitting in God's face. And they don't care—worse, they hand out prizes to those who do the worst things best!
>
> Romans 1:28-32 MSG[1]

Man's fallen nature doesn't draw him to God; it drives him deeper into sin. The consequence of a sinful lifestyle facilitates suffering. God doesn't delight in the suffering of mankind. Suffering came about as a result of mankind's decision to obey Satan instead of God. Much of suffering continues as a result of a lifestyle of sinful choices. Paul expressed it was the goodness and grace of God that work toward our repentance, not God sending suffering.

2. Though man's original disobedience brought about suffering, God made provision for, and is presently working toward, reversing the consequences of man's fall. Ultimate victory over suffering, though not yet experienced, is assured by Scripture:

> And I saw a new heaven and a new earth: for the first heaven and the first earth were passed away; and there was no more sea. And I John saw the holy city, new Jerusalem, coming down from God out of heaven, prepared as a bride adorned for her husband. And I

heard a great voice out of heaven saying, Behold, the tabernacle of God is with men, and he will dwell with them, and they shall be his people, and God himself shall be with them, and be their God. And God shall wipe away all tears from their eyes, and there shall be no more death, neither sorrow, nor crying, neither shall there be any more pain: for the former things are passed away.
Revelation 21:1-4

3. If freedom from suffering was linked to salvation, this would be a manipulative ploy of God to get all to serve Him without caring about Him. This was the relationship Satan accused God of arranging with Job. Conversely, we should serve God out of love and choice in spite of our suffering.

> Then Satan answered the Lord, and said, Doth Job fear God for nought? Hast not thou made an hedge about him, and about his house, and about all that he hath on every side? thou hast blessed the work of his hands, and his substance is increased in the land. But put forth thine hand now, and touch all that he hath, and he will curse thee to thy face.
Job 1:9-11

We shouldn't live for God on the basis of what He does for us, rather, on the basis of who He is: the God of the universe, our Creator, and our Savior. We recognize we are a part of His dominion and He truly cares for us. We realize He does kind things for us out of love, but we shouldn't interpret the bad things that happen to us as indicative of His lack of love or that He sent suffering as punishment.

4. Suffering strengthens us. We understand that some suffering may be allowed of the Lord for our best interest or with an eternal purpose far beyond our ability to realize. We develop through suffering; otherwise, we would be spiritually and emotionally weak. A doting God, who deflects all suffering from us, would produce spoiled children. Suffering serves, as exercise does for the physical

man, as a means of strengthening the emotional and spiritual man. Just as physical exercise strengthens the muscles, suffering strengthens the spiritual, mental, and emotional man.

No one was more qualified to speak, nor has spoken more succinctly regarding suffering, than Helen Keller. With her body locked in a prison of darkness and silence, her mind escaped to paint light into the darkness and fill the silence with poetic verse. Her life could have been confined to barnyard grubbing, but with the guidance of a loving teacher, she soared in celestial tranquility and left literary gems that have inspired millions. Regarding suffering she wrote, "Character cannot be developed in ease and quiet. Only through experience of trial and suffering can the soul be strengthened, ambition inspired, and success achieved.[2]

> For whom the Lord loveth he chasteneth, and scourgeth every son whom he receiveth. If ye endure chastening, God dealeth with you as with sons, for what son is he whom the father chasteneth not? But if ye be without chastisement whereof all are partakers, then are ye bastards, and not sons. Furthermore we have had fathers of our flesh which corrected us, and we gave them reverence: shall we not much rather be in subjection unto the Father of spirits, and live? For they verily for a few days chastened us after their own pleasure; but he for our profit, that we might be partakers of his holiness. Now no chastening for the present seemeth to be joyous, but grievous: nevertheless afterward it yieldeth the peaceable fruit of righteousness unto them which are exercised thereby.
>
> Hebrews 12:6-11

5. All suffering isn't sent by the Lord to teach some spiritual lesson such as faith or obedience. Most suffering is a result of the circumstances of life. But when this happens, God is obligated by Scriptural promises to enter into the picture and bring something good out of the suffering. "And we know that all things work

together for good to them that love God, to them who are the called according to his purpose" (Romans 8:28).

6. Though God allows suffering, and He is working on eliminating it, in the meantime, He chooses to join us in our suffering. No matter the pain, He understands. He sees every tear that falls. At any moment He is capable of demanding, "That's enough!"

The "why" question is softened if we understand God's position in our suffering. Where is God when we need Him? He's right beside us, or better still, He's within us, through the abiding presence of His Spirit. He walks with us through the valley. He stays with us in the fiery-furnace trial. He remains with us in the lions' den throughout the long, lonely night. He suffers with us in our prison captivity. And though we may feel forsaken, He lingers with us in our Gethsemane, walks the Via Delarosa with us, and hangs on a cross beside us. "And, behold I am with thee, and will keep thee in all places whither thou goest, and will bring thee again into this land; for I will not leave thee, until I have done that which I have spoken to thee of" (Genesis 28:15). "When thou passest through the waters, I will be with thee; and through the rivers they shall not overflow thee; when thou walkest through the fire, thou shalt not be burned; neither shall the flame kindle upon thee" (Isaiah 43:2).

We have an open invitation to go to Him with our needs. When life is out of control, we are invited to come to Him and petition His help.

> For we have not an high priest which cannot be touched with the feeling of our infirmities; but was in all points tempted like as we are, yet without sin. Let us therefore come boldly unto the throne of grace, that we may obtain mercy, and find grace to help in time of need.
>
> Hebrews 4:15-16

The book of Job, along with a host of lessons of other Bible characters, tells us God encompasses the fiercest storm, not only piloting our ship to its destination, but when necessary, commanding the winds and waves to calm. Our ultimate victory is assured, not by how we feel, but by what we know from His promises made to us. His promises extend beyond life itself. They are eternal. A defeat is not the end, for God always has another move. Even death isn't final; it is the door back into God's eternal presence.

I love the following story. It's recorded in various versions in a multitude of sermons. I haven't located its original author; so I use it, indebted to someone.

> Two men visiting an art gallery studied an unusual painting of a man playing chess with the devil. The devil's ear-to-ear grin told the story. The title of the painting, Checkmate, indicated the game was over. The devil had won. His opponent had no more moves.
>
> One of the men observing the painting suddenly stepped back and announced: "It's wrong! We have to contact the painter. He has to rename the painting."
>
> "Why?" His companion didn't understand.
>
> "Because it's not checkmate. The king still has one more move."

So it is with the Lord; He always has another move. As helpless as Job seemed, God wasn't worried. Not once. He never runs out of moves.

Points of Discussion

The Bible describes Job's verbal response regarding the devastating loss of his family and possessions, but what might his thoughts have been?

In what ways does Satan maximize the pain of suffering?

Discuss how Divine punishment for Adam's transgression brought suffering, and yet God should not be blamed for mankind's lingering suffering.

How can a loving God come alongside us during our suffering while allowing the suffering to continue?

Chapter 5

The Questions of Suffering

> How long wilt thou forget me, O LORD? for ever?
> How long wilt thou hide thy face from me?
>
> Psalms 13:1

We frequently ask two questions, often in sequence: "Why, Lord? Why me, Lord?" To the first question, we offered some direction in chapter one. Now let's give consideration to the second: "Why me?"

Does God single us out for specific suffering? If so, the question "Why me?" is justifiable. First, let's understand God isn't intimidated by our questions, for even Christ questioned, "My God, my God, why hast thou forsaken me?" (Matthew 27:46). Christ's example shows us questioning is a normal cognitive process, and it shows us the proper attitude in questing God. Christ wasn't denying or challenging. He quoted from Old Testament Scripture: "My God, my God, why hast thou forsaken me? why art thou so far from helping me, and from the words of my roaring?" (Psalms 22:1). This shows Christ wasn't denying His faith; he was affirming it with a question amplified by His suffering.

God specifically singled out Job for suffering. "And the Lord said unto Satan, Hast thou considered my servant Job, that there is none like him in the earth, a perfect and an upright man, one that feareth God, and escheweth evil?" (Job 1:8).

The Lord actually initiated Job's testing from Satan. And though we don't necessarily know why, a question to which Job himself probably never found an answer, we need some direction as to the question, "Why me?"

Throughout the book of Job we encounter several questions. In chapter three, Job asks the "why" question no less than five times. In the presence of his three friends Job questioned, "Why me? Why does it have to be? Why could I not have died instead?" This seems a rather normal response to the suffering endured by Job. Since there's no measuring rod for the severity of suffering, we can't categorize those who may or may not be justified in asking "Why?" All who suffer probably wonder why. Some verbalize their thoughts, and some record their ramblings in personal journals. Many excellent books exist that offer coping techniques. The Bible is my recommended source for inspiration regarding surviving suffering. Because of Job's recorded sufferings and his questions, along with other Biblical accounts, we can learn positive coping methods by reading the Bible narratives relating to suffering. The Bible answers many common questions regarding suffering.

1. Though suffering is a result of man's original sin, it is not necessarily a result of personal sin. Many operate from a flawed theology that says if you suffer you must have done something wrong, and if you suffer severely you must have done something terribly wrong. This was the attitude of Job's friends (commonly referred to as Job's comforters). Sin does bring consequences, but to say all suffering occurs because one has sinned, and God is sending punishment, isn't Scriptural. John's gospel records Jesus' response to this type of faulty theology.

> And as Jesus passed by, he saw a man who was blind from birth. And his disciples asked him, saying, Master, who did sin, this man, or his parents, that he was born blind? Jesus answered, Neither hath this man sinned, nor his parents: but that the works of God should be made manifest in him.
> John 9:1-3

It's always prudent to evaluate one's shortcomings; likewise, it's unwise to berate oneself regarding every adverse situation. If sin is the obvious culprit then repentance is in order, and grace is the answer. Obviously, healing is selective. It is possible but is dependent upon divine consideration: God sometimes chooses not to heal an individual. In contrast, forgiveness of sins is an absolute promise to the repentant heart. God made provision for anyone whose suffering is a direct result of personal sin:

> Is any sick among you? let him call for the elders of the church; and let them pray over him, anointing him with oil in the name of the Lord: And the prayer of faith shall save the sick, and the Lord shall raise him up; and if he have committed sins, they shall be forgiven him. Confess your faults one to another, and pray one for another, that ye may be healed. The effectual fervent prayer of a righteous man availeth much.
>
> James 5:14-16

2. Righteous living doesn't prevent all suffering. Living godly has numerous advantages in this life and especially in the life to come. Still, it doesn't shield mortal man from ordinary situations of life. Suffering results from a number of conditions, particularly the laws of nature. "But doesn't God control the forces of nature?" we ask. Though nature is a part of God's creation, it suffers from the calamity of the curse of sin. And though God can control nature, He doesn't always choose to do so. Divine interventions of nature are miracles. There are a host of recorded miracles in the Bible, but these aren't the norm. Contrariwise, God doesn't always choose to work the miraculous. Tragedies caused by nature should normally be viewed as unfortunate circumstances rather than divine judgment. The wheels of nature (storms, tornadoes, cyclones, floods, and droughts) keep grinding. The righteous, along with the wicked, confined to the earth, unfortunately, are often in harm's way.

To prevent natural disasters form happening to the righteous, God would have to create two sets of natural laws, one for the wicked and another for the righteous. He doesn't have such. As the rain falls upon the just and the unjust, tornadoes descend indiscriminately upon many. This occurred more vividly to me when a tornado struck a church congregation whose pastor was a personal friend. These were good people. Faithful people. Loving people. Because of the good the church complex represents, we assume it to be a safe haven from natural disasters. Yet this church building proved otherwise. A lady who left her home and sought shelter in the church facilities was killed, and the pastor's daughter was severely injured. Neither the church building nor its inhabitants received exemption from this natural catastrophe. God does choose many times to protect the righteous. Each time this occurs is another miracle. For this we give Him thanks, but we shouldn't accuse Him when disaster strikes. We mustn't subscribe to an attitude of demanding special attention. This seemed to be the philosophy of Job's wife: righteous living always receives righteous rewards, and unrighteous living receives retribution. Job offered an explanation: "But he said unto her, Thou speakest as one of the foolish women speaketh. What? shall we receive good at the hand of God, and shall we not receive evil? In all this did not Job sin with his lips" (Job 2:10).

Job gave the right explanation to his wife, though it may have been difficult for him in practical application, especially after an elapse of time without any relief from his pain. In the end Job assures us though life may not seem fair, God is just, His decisions are right, and our submission to God's purpose is always best. It's a faith to which we should aspire, not an understanding which we can always explain. In contrast to the account of Adam and Eve in the garden, Job did not succumb to the influence of his wife; the outcome is obvious. He and his wife weren't cast from God's presence; conversely, they remained in God's favor, and when the storm passed they received His manifold blessings. The blessings that came never erased the pain of the loss of their children, but the blessings allowed them to know they were in God's favor.

3. Much suffering is caused by the errors of man, not the oversight, unkindness, or inability of God. Tragically, much suffering is a result of common sense errors. God doesn't send heart attacks; conversely they often happen as a result of poor habits. A group of teens, trying for a good time, zoom along at an excessive speed and crash into a bridge abutment. This isn't a curse of God or negligence on His part; it has to do with poor decisions. Man

is knowledgeable of the dangers of alcohol and drugs, but he still challenges the risk. This is not God's doing. Still, when tragedy strikes close to home we tend to ask "Why?" That isn't necessarily challenging God so much as it is the cognitive process at work. The danger comes when we blame God, sometimes shutting Him out of the reasoning process.

4. Some tragedies are a result of man's God-given freedom. Freedom of choice was granted man in the Garden of Eden and has never been revoked. As a youngster, my family lived in an isolated community in Appalachia Kentucky. The cost of living was extremely low; the risk was sometimes quite high. There were no policemen, no firemen, no doctors, but there were thieves, arsonists, and lots of rattlesnakes. Natural disasters left us with little refuge. We survived the tragedy of two floods, both times forced to evacuate our home by the rising tide of nature. We lost most everything except our lives, the clothes on our back, and a few items we managed to move to higher ground. We could be sad for losing everything or grateful for having our lives spared. Here again is the freedom to choose.

Our suffering caused by these floods was not God's doing; it was my dad's doing by a decision he made. A flood had devastated the community a number of years prior to the building of this house. Dad was somewhat of a horse trader, and when the house came up for sale, his trading skills kicked in, and he discouraged a potential buyer by warning him the house stood in the flood zone. I use the term stood, for the house was built upon stilts. That should've been a clue about the potential for future flooding, but for some reason, Dad had his heart set on this particular house. When the buyer backed out, Dad made his lowball offer, and we moved into our new home. Twice in five years the floodwaters came. It may seem God sent the flood to punish Dad for his unscrupulous deal, but I doubt that. Too many wonderful neighbors, and hundreds of others along the North Fork of the Kentucky River, had their lives interrupted and homes destroyed by the floods for this to be a single punishment upon my dad.

After the second flood, instead of blaming God, Dad moved us to another location. That, too, was his personal choice. There have been additional consequences, good and bad, that came from that choice to relocate his family.

Choices have the potential for prosperity or disaster. Still, prosperity isn't necessarily the stamp of God's approval, and disaster isn't necessarily God's punishment for sin. The freedom to choose is more significant than the consequences of choices we make. Some societies don't have this freedom of choice. Ask anyone who has lived under communist oppression, where choices are removed and life is dictated, if they would rather have the right to choose, even though it comes with certain risks. Further, a person who refuses to make choices about life falls into some psychological category of abnormal behavior. Life is full of choices. Sadly, many erroneously blame God for the outcome of choices, and in so doing they sometimes make foolish decisions, such as blaming Him, becoming angry at Him, and shutting Him out of their lives.

5. Some suffering is caused by an attack from Satan. Satan, a wicked spirit being, is loose in the world to roam and wreak havoc. This was not the Lord's doing; it happened as a result of man's transgression in the garden. Prior to Adam and Eve's wrongdoing, they were in a favored position with God, and Satan had no control over them. They gave up that unique position with God when they sinned and became subjected to Satan's sway. We are descendants of an enslaved race. Our owner, the devil, is a barbaric taskmaster. He is constantly at work among the inhabitants of planet earth. "And the Lord said unto Satan, Whence comest thou? Then Satan answered the Lord, and said, From going to and fro in the earth, and from walking up and down in it" (Job 1:7).

Prior to the fall, mankind operated in a realm of authority over sin and Satan. Post-Eden changed such. Though not without God's daily fellowship and warning regarding disobedience, mankind succumbed to the deceptive promises of Satan. God still offers an element of protection for those living under the grace of Calvary, but carnality plays a convincing role in our decision- making process, and Satan continues to harass all of mankind. "Be sober, be vigilant; because your adversary the devil, as a roaring lion, walketh about, seeking whom he may devour" (I Peter 5:8). Though the believer isn't exempt from the attacks and temptations of Satan, the believer is

Suffering With Purpose

assured of God's provision to overcome Satan. This is accomplished through God's inner-working power. "Ye are of God, little children, and have overcome them: because greater is he that is in you, than he that is in the world" (I John 4:4).

God's love for us is unfathomable. He proved this by Calvary's sacrifice. As Christians, our debt of sin was paid in full by Christ's atoning death. Still, we aren't exempt from suffering and temptation by the adversary. These are part of the process of redemption. We must patiently endure the process. All consequence of sin will be reversed in heaven. This is God's promise.

> And I heard a great voice out of heaven saying, Behold, the tabernacle of God is with men, and he will dwell with them, and they shall be his people, and God himself shall be with them, and be their God. And God shall wipe away all tears from their eyes; and there shall be no more death, neither sorrow, nor crying, neither shall there be any more pain: for the former things are passed away.
>
> Revelation 21:3-4

After the Garden of Eden debacle, Satan claimed all of mankind by virtue of humanity's inherited sinful nature. Though a newborn isn't responsible for Adam's sin, that child will eventually sin due to an inherited and iniquitous nature. Mankind carries a recessive gene of wickedness, which when coupled with opportunity and temptation, produces sinful deeds. Christ's sacrificial offering of His sinless self offers mankind access to a spiritual new birth. The new birth allows freedom from Satan's control. Christ doesn't leave His own at Satan's mercy; rather, Christ, knowing our weaknesses, will not allow Satan to touch us without a meaningful reason, a limited time frame, and never beyond our ability to endure. To touch a child of God, Satan must infiltrate God's omniscient shield of ownership. This can only happen by Divine permission. In the story of Job, Satan had to obtain permission to afflict Job. "And the LORD said unto Satan, Behold, he is in thine hand; but save his life" (Job 2:6). If Satan is allowed to assault, the child of God can remain confident in Christ's promises of ultimate victory.

> Whom resist stedfast in the faith, knowing that the same afflictions are accomplished in your brethren that are in the world. But the God of all grace, who hath called us unto his eternal glory by Christ Jesus, after that ye have suffered a while, make you perfect, stablish, strengthen, settle you.
>
> I Peter 5:9-10

God, out of daily mercy, closely monitors our suffering. "It is of the Lord's mercies that we are not consumed, because his compassions fail not. They are new every morning: great is thy faithfulness" (Lamentations 3:22-23). God understands our frailty while He works on strengthening our faith. This is why Satan had to obtain permission from the Lord before he could harm Job. It may appear God and Satan struggled for dominance over Job's life, but this is not the case. God was confident in Job's faith: with or without His blessing. It is significant to understand we are not caught helplessly between the struggle of two superpowers: God and Satan. Conversely, there's only one superpower: Jesus Christ. "And Jesus came and spake unto them, saying, All power is given unto me in heaven and in earth" (Matthew 28:18). Satan, using the same deception ploy he used in the garden, attempts to undermine God's supremacy. The Apostle Paul wrote to the Colossian Christians, whose faith was challenged by heretical teachings infiltrating their membership. He reminded them of Christ's creative and redemptive power. "For by him were all things created, that are in heaven, and that are in earth, visible and invisible, whether they be thrones, or dominions, or principalities, or powers: all things were created by him, and for him" (Colossians 1:16). The expanded verses are noteworthy:

> That ye might walk worthy of the Lord unto all pleasing, being fruitful in every good work, and increasing in the knowledge of God; Strengthened with all might, according to his glorious power, unto all patience and longsuffering with joyfulness; Giving thanks unto the Father, which hath made us

Suffering With Purpose

meet to be partakers of the inheritance of the saints in light: Who hath delivered us from the power of darkness, and hath translated us into the kingdom of his dear Son: In whom we have redemption through his blood, even the forgiveness of sins: Who is the image of the invisible God, the firstborn of every creature: For by him were all things created, that are in heaven, and that are in earth, visible and invisible, whether they be thrones, or dominions, or principalities, or powers: all things were created by him, and for him: And he is before all things, and by him all things consist. And he is the head of the body, the church: who is the beginning, the firstborn from the dead; that in all things he might have the preeminence. For it pleased the Father that in him should all fulness dwell; And, having made peace through the blood of his cross, by him to reconcile all things unto himself; by him, I say, whether they be things in earth, or things in heaven. And you, that were sometime alienated and enemies in your mind by wicked works, yet now hath he reconciled In the body of his flesh through death, to present you holy and unblameable and unreproveable in his sight: If ye continue in the faith grounded and settled, and be not moved away from the hope of the gospel, which ye have heard, and which was preached to every creature which is under heaven; whereof I Paul am made a minister;

Colossians 1:10-23

The struggle with Satan continues because Satan is trying to prevent the inevitable: his unavoidable eternal judgment. In the meantime, we who truly trust Christ, though we may momentarily question suffering, must learn to accept the good and the bad that comes our way. This truly is to love Christ. Anything less, such as complaining or blaming, is to have an insufficient faith in Jesus Christ. Religion becomes nothing more than bargain hunting, serving Christ because He protects us, rather than out of love for Him and appreciation for what He's already done at Calvary.

"Why me, Lord?" Perhaps we'll never know the answer this side of eternity. Job never did. We may never see clearly the reason for our particular suffering, but we can experience Christ's love, which supersedes anything He could do for us. His love was expressed, not in words alone, but by submission to a rugged cross on a wind-swept hill long ago, where He joined mankind in suffering and gave hope to all who suffer but maintain faith in His atoning sacrifice.

The book of Job doesn't necessarily explain the why of suffering; rather, it paints a portrait of all mankind, born in a world of suffering and uncertainty, and it offers us directives and hope to survive the storm. Job clung to his faith in God, not always doing or saying the right things but remaining steadfast in his love toward God. He blazed a trail for us to follow. The trail leads through the tangle and snares of an uncertain present. It is not a meaningless mess; contrariwise, the traveler realizes God traverses this trail. To follow Him is assurance the narrow path will eventually open into a field of favor and opportunity. Or better still, heaven.

Points of Discussion

Discuss how the "why" question can be both negative and positive.

How could God justify allowing Satan to harm Job?

Since suffering is a result of sin, why did God allow mankind the power to choose instead of creating him with the ability to respond only as God desired?

Discuss why God allows Satan to attack and sometimes harm His creation.

Chapter 6

Response to Suffering

> … weeping may endure for a night, but joy cometh in the morning.
>
> Psalms 30:1

Prevention of adversity is impossible. Many have tried but failed. They're generally noted for their eccentricity in a negative manner. Their obsessive and compulsive behavior often creates multiple side effects. Despite all their efforts, adversity eventually catches up. No one can cocoon in a problem-free bubble. Sooner or later calamity strikes. Since Adam's fall we've been enslaved by sin's curse and affected adversely by the evil spirit world that dominates terra firma. Satan continues to claim us by virtue of our disobedience to God, which renders us vulnerable to his devices. As Satan attacked Job he continues to assault mankind even to the present hour. He'll do so until the Lord commands His angel to bind Satan and lock him away.

> And I saw an angel come down from heaven, having the key of the bottomless pit and a great chain in his hand. And he laid hold on the dragon, that old serpent, which is the Devil, and Satan, and bound him a thousand years, And cast him into the bottomless pit, and shut him up, and set a seal upon him, that he should deceive the nations no more, till the thousand years should be fulfilled: and after that he must be

loosed a little season. And the devil that deceived them was cast into the lake of fire and brimstone, where the beast and the false prophet are, and shall be tormented day and night for ever and ever.

Revelation 20:1-3, 20

Through the ages Satan has come against God's best. When we consider the list, no one is exempt from being singled out for Satan's attack. This is not to suggest Satan is omnipresent, ever present to tempt all of humanity at the same time. Temptations come in luring forms such as mass media, or they may be subtler, such as a small inner voice of carnality. Still, you and I may be singled out for a direct attack of Satan, or we may be accosted by one of the fallen angels whose plight is the same as Satan's, but who are his subjects in an organized evil empire.

> And you hath he quickened, who were dead in trespasses and sins; Wherein in time past ye walked according to the course of this world, according to the prince of the power of the air, the spirit that now worketh in the children of disobedience: Among whom also we all had our conversation in times past in the lusts of our flesh, fulfilling the desires of the flesh and of the mind; and were by nature the children of wrath, even as others.
>
> Ephesians 2:1-3

Scripture is plain in its warning regarding the possibility of a direct attack from Satan or an evil spirit doing his bidding. We have numerous examples of those, representing various ranks in life, who were the direct target of Satan. These Biblical examples offer caution to us:

> ***The Religious, Joshua the High Priest:*** "And he shewed me Joshua the high priest standing before the angel of the Lord, and Satan standing at his right hand to resist him" (Zechariah 3:1).

The Statesman, David the King: "And Satan stood up against Israel, and provoked David to number Israel" (I Chronicles 21:1).

The Perfect, Christ: "Then was Jesus led up of the Spirit into the wilderness to be tempted of the devil" (Matthew 4:1).

The Apostles, Judas and Peter: "And supper being ended, the devil having now put into the heart of Judas Iscariot, Simon's son, to betray him" (John 13:2). "And the Lord said, Simon, Simon, behold, Satan hath desired to have you, that he may sift you as wheat" (Luke 22:31).

The Ordinary, You and me: Be sober, be vigilant; because your adversary the devil, as a roaring lion, walketh about, seeking whom he may devour" (I Peter 5:8).

We are no match against Satan and his forces. To believe we have personal strength and resourcefulness to overcome and outmaneuver Satan is arrogance, ignorance, or both. Such deception is one of the strongest weapons in Satan's arsenal. He sets a trap and waits for us to step into it. He springs upon us when we least expect it. He lures us using our own desires. His ways are tried and proven. He outlasts and is unscrupulous. Of angelic origin, he operates in a realm beyond mortal man's ability. On the other hand, we aren't defenseless. Think of it as a trip to the zoo. Though numerous animals at the zoo are capable and genetically designed to kill humans, visitors are perfectly safe so long as they follow a few guidelines printed along the way.

Do not climb over the wall.

Do not stick your arms inside the cage.

Do not feed the animals.

In the midst of dangerous animals, visitors at the zoo are safer than the wild game hunter equipped with the most sophisticated weapons. Why? The jungle has few rules and many unrestrained conditions. In contrast, the zoo has a few rules for the visitors and many restraints upon the animals. Likewise, God (dare I call Him our zookeeper) hasn't abandoned us in a spiritual jungle full of wild and preying animals. There are two reasons we are safer in His protection than we are visiting a zoo: God has established guidelines for us to follow that assure our safety; God has established boundaries that Satan cannot cross. At the zoo the lions are caged. The elephants have barriers that contain them. The snakes are encased. Likewise, Satan is corralled by God's design. Though Satan isn't caged, he is controlled. When Satan attacks, it is with limitations because of our God-designated defense system. What is this defense? Trust in God's Word and submission to God's plan. At all times we have the Scriptural invitation to enter Christ's presence for help. "Let us therefore come boldly unto the throne of grace, that we may obtain mercy, and find grace to help in time of need" (Hebrews 4:16). Further, we can appeal to His death on Calvary's cross, recognizing Jesus' death won our victory. Through Jesus' name we have authority to resist Satan from our lives. This isn't arrogance; it is confidence that the zookeeper of our soul will rush to defend us against any dangerous animal that has escaped his cage. To resist Satan in the name of Jesus is to call upon the rightful protection the zookeeper offers. "Yet Michael the archangel, when contending with the devil he disputed about the body of Moses, durst not bring against him a railing accusation, but said, The Lord rebuke thee" (Jude 9). "Submit yourselves therefore to God. Resist the devil, and he will flee from you" (James 4:7).

    The danger zone in which we too often live makes us ill-prepared for suffering. We operate with too few prayers, hurried Bible reading, and inconsistency in our overall Christian commitment. We take far better care of our physical man than we do the spiritual man. It's common practice to eat three meals a day and drink six to eight glasses of water. We are well aware of the physical consequences of going on too little sleep. However, we are very inconsistent in taking care of the spiritual man. We slip in a prayer here and there throughout the week and read a few Bible verses to ease a nagging conscience. With this type of spiritual inconsistency, why are we surprised when we're overwhelmed by life's curveball or Satan's sudden attack? Though we can't prevent Satan's attacks, we can better prepare to face them by consistency in the basics of Christianity: prayer and Bible study. Job's life exemplifies proper preparation for Satan's unexpected attack.

> There was a man in the land of Uz, whose name was Job; and that man was perfect and upright, and one that feared God, and eschewed evil. And it was so, when the days of their feasting were gone about, that Job sent and sanctified them, and rose up early in the morning, and offered burnt offerings according to the number of them all: for Job said, It may be that my sons have sinned, and cursed God in their hearts. Thus did Job continually.
>
> Job 1:1,5

Perfect! Upright! Feared God! Shunned evil! From these descriptive words it is obvious Job loved God and did his best to serve Him. What a formula for prevention! Yet, adversity came. Not just a thunderstorm; rather, it was a cyclone of calamity, an avalanche of adversity. His preparation didn't prevent suffering nor make it less severe. But a life geared toward God better equips us for a first response when adversity comes and keeps us through the drawn-out battle.

The Response of Faith

The Christian faith is not designed to always make us feel better; it is designed make us a better person instead of becoming bitter when confronted with adversity. An article by the Mayo Clinic staff expresses the significance of the principle of forgiveness in contrast to bearing a grudge:

> Nearly everyone has been hurt by the actions or words of another. Perhaps your mother criticized your parenting skills, your colleague sabotaged a project or your partner had an affair. These wounds can leave you with lasting feelings of anger, bitterness or even vengeance — but if you don't practice forgiveness,

you might be the one who pays most dearly. By embracing forgiveness, you can also embrace peace, hope, gratitude and joy.[1]

Long before the study of the psychological effects of negative emotions, the Creator gave instruction regarding the consequences of negative attitudes in approaching life. Faith in God's goodness toward humanity is essential for spiritual health. Consistency in spiritual disciplines includes prayer, Bible reading, and worship to God. Translated into modern Christianity, spiritual discipline includes not only prayer and Bible reading but also church attendance, personal ministry to others, and involvement in small groups that offer spiritual support. Though not an exhaustive list, all these are faith builders. Faith is the basic building block of Christianity. To have a strong faith base is comparable to the training essential for any profession: military, first responders, or kindergarten teachers. No matter how the situation may unravel, you are emotionally prepared to weather the storm. In the secular world we call it "staying confidence". It's staying on track by operating in the manner in which you've been professionally trained. In a spiritual sense it is called faith: a trust in the character, power, promises, and love of Christ.

How we feel often, erroneously, determines our faith. We feel good so we have faith. Tragedy strikes, and we feel like quitting. When the pain eases, we feel we can make it. When trouble returns we feel weak. The problem? Faith isn't about how we feel; it's about the God who loves and watches over us in every situation. Suffering may well trump feeling, for suffering often dictates how we feel. We dare not be dominated by how we feel; rather, we must respond by what we know about God through His Word. Suffering doesn't trump faith; conversely, faith outlasts suffering. Interestingly, in our relationship toward God, Bible scholars point out the Greek word for feeling is used sparingly, but knowledge is used multiple times. Faith that God is going to help should not be predicated upon how I feel; rather, it should be based upon what God's Word says. Faith offered by the Bible is based upon an understanding of God's character. A deep trust develops within the believer's heart because of what the Bible says regarding God. This is true faith. Human emotions, or feelings, are fickle, controlled by chemicals within the body, which are strongly affected by overwhelming circumstances, both real and perceived. The outcome varies but is predictable: fear, flight, depression, joy, and a host of emotions, depending upon the circumstances. Mood swings can be so extreme that a trip to the mailbox, where one receives a bill, can make one instantly blue, or receiving a long awaited tax check makes one immediately ecstatic.

Too often we are ill-prepared spiritually to handle small problems, let alone catastrophes. We haven't participated in the spiritual drills that equip us for the real battle. We often realize our inadequacies during a tragic situation. Unlike professionals, we seldom prepare for tragedy. For example, firemen are trained to deal with fires. The untrained may run from the fire, or run into the fire, controlled by emotions (fear of the flames, or love for someone trapped inside the flames). The fireman knows what to do and what not to do. This discipline is drilled into him. The fireman's response may be the opposite of what an untrained and emotionally charged person may do. Likewise, the practice of spiritual disciplines allows one to operate according to the wisdom of the Bible, which not only is always right but also is a different realm than that in which the emotional man operates. Emotions are held in check in the realm of faith. Faith is not a pie in the sky mentality, not a name-it-claim-it revival fervor. Faith believes and practices what the Bible says.

> My son, forget not my law; but let thine heart keep my commandments: For length of days, and long life, and peace, shall they add to thee. Let not mercy and truth forsake thee: bind them about thy neck; write them upon the table of thine heart: So shalt thou find favour and good understanding in the sight of God and man. Trust in the LORD with all thine heart; and lean not unto thine own understanding. In all thy ways acknowledge him, and he shall direct thy paths. Be not wise in thine own eyes: fear the LORD, and depart from evil. It shall be health to thy navel, and marrow to thy bones.
>
> Proverbs 3:1-8

In a letter to the first century Roman church Paul expressed the process of acquiring faith. The acquisition of faith is associated with the discipline of studying the Bible. "So then faith cometh by hearing, and hearing by the word of God" (Romans 10:17). The Bible is the Christian's sole source of faith. No matter what the doctor says, society does, or nature produces, God is the final authority. The psalmist stated: "Thy word have I hid in mine heart, that I might not sin against thee" (Psalms 119:11). To know and to do what the Bible says is to do the right thing, the God thing.

The Discipline of Prayer

Job consistently practiced the basic spiritual discipline of prayer. Prayer played a major role in his life, for Job did not have the Bible to instruct him since the Bible was not yet written. Though the ancients treasured their oral traditions, the written text would not appear until Moses. The account of Job predated the written Scripture by many years. Job was unaware that later, in the written text, he would be a central figure exemplifying faith. We now have the Bible, with its many characters and how they lived: the right way and the wrong, the good decisions and the bad. Job's response to adversity offers us a pattern to follow when confronted by adversity. His disciplined life of prayer perpetuated his exemplary response. Consider his response to the tragic news of his horrific loss.

> Then Job arose, and rent his mantle, and shaved his head, and fell down upon the ground, and worshipped, And said Naked came I out of my mother's womb, and naked shall I return thither: the Lord gave, and the Lord hath taken away; blessed be the name of the Lord. In all this Job sinned not, nor charged God foolishly. Then said his wife unto him, Dost thou still retain thine integrity? curse God, and die. But he said unto her, Thou speakest as one of the foolish women speaketh. What? shall we receive good at the hand of God, and shall we not receive evil? In all this did not Job sin with his lips.
>
> Job 1:20-22; 2:9-10

Emotional Response

The response to crisis is extremely important. Response can be one of despair or one of faith. It can be a door through which we begin a journey of optimism; conversely, it can be a door that locks us inside prison walls of despair. It may determine whether we give up or keep going, seek strength through prayer or through pills. Job's initial response set a pattern for his ongoing reaction to suffering. His response is a positive pattern for us to follow. Consider how Job responded to his tragedy. He rent his mantle and shaved his head: a sign of overwhelming grief. Grief, with all its anguish, is a positive and natural response to losing someone or something that is dear to us: a parent, a child, a friend, a job, our health, a home. Grief isn't a weak response; it has meaningful purpose. To grieve isn't expressing a lack of faith; it's a normal response to loss. Jesus wept at the tomb of His friend Lazarus. Though Christ had already proclaimed Himself to be the resurrection, He still grieved for His friend's departure from this life. Though God Incarnate, He possessed human emotions. The Prophet Isaiah described Him as "a man of sorrows, and acquainted with grief" (Isaiah 53:3). Christ stood at the grave to rebuke death's grip on Lazarus; still, He shed tears of sorrow, a natural response to grief. Research has determined that tears act as a release valve that prevents the build-up of stress-producing chemicals within the body. Such relief is necessary because stress causes physical harm if not dealt with properly.

Much has been written about the various stages of grief. Grief is a positive response in dealing with loss, and to grieve properly is essential for emotional healing. Commonly accepted stages of grief reaction include: denial, anger, guilt, depression, and resolution (acceptance). To grieve is not to dishonor God. It is not sin. Neither is grief an indication of emotional weakness, though grief may resemble clinical depression. Notable Christian authors of an excellent Psychology textbook write the following regarding grief reactions:

> The grief reactions normally experienced by persons suffering a significant loss are not clinical depressions. A grief reaction can turn into depression, however, if

short-circuited. The five stages experienced by most people who grieve, described by Kübler-Ross (1969), should be regarded as healthy safeguards against chronic depression.[2]

The concern regarding grief is that the individual fails to work through the stages and becomes stuck in a particular stage, failing to arrive at and experience the final stage of acceptance. Letting go takes a great deal of faith. Perhaps that makes it very difficult for the unbeliever: death is so final. For the believer it is a journey of acceptance of the present state, but with a Biblical hope of the life to come. This process of grief reaction is a work of faith.

Human Response

When approaching suffering from a Christian perspective, too often we fail to acknowledge our humanity. Our expectations for ourselves and others have an unrealistic, even super-human, quality to them. Because of such expectations we misinterpret being human as being sinful, when in actuality, being human is being what God created. It is normal to be human, and being human and being sinful are not necessarily the same. We should accept our humanity but guard it from carnality. There is a difference between being human and being carnal.

Being human is to experience all the emotions endowed by our Creator. Carnality is to experience those emotions in a selfish and sensual manner: thinking only of self or desiring pleasures forbidden by Scripture. The Bible doesn't forbid us from being happy over a financial blessing we receive, but it does forbid us from taking the last dollar a debtor may have to feed his family in order that we might indulge in a Caribbean cruise. Christ's instruction shows the difference: "He answereth and saith unto them, He that hath two coats, let him impart to him that hath none; and he that hath meat, let him do likewise" (Luke 3:11). It's okay to have two coats until you see someone freezing because they have none. To have two coats is a blessing. To be selfish regarding the second coat is to respond in a carnal manner; this response is sin.

Job's wife has been condemned as the irreligious spouse. We quickly judge her as responding sinfully when she very well could have been responding from human emotions. We give little consideration to the thought that she, too, had suffered loss alongside her husband. She had to advance through the stages of grief. More than likely she was struggling somewhere in the stages of grief when the Scripture records her negative words. Somewhere along her journey of suffering, possibly she came to grips with her anger toward God, to a realization she was falsely accusing Him and, perhaps, accusing her husband. At some point, to purposefully retain anger toward God is to slip from being human to being a carnal person. The difference may seem a fine line, but over time one's carnality is quite recognizable. I've seen many angry at God months after the death of a loved one; I've seen some angry at God years after the death of a loved one. There is a difference: the first is being human; the latter may well be carnality.

Through all the unbelievable heartache, it seems Job's wife worked through the stages of grief. In the end she remained with Job, raising another family and sharing in God's blessing.

When we walk through the stages of grief, feeling angry or depressed, we have not lost out with God. "Why have you forsaken me?" Jesus cried into the brassy sky. That was a human response to pain, not a carnal response challenging God's character. Christ is our example, more than anyone else, and He, like no one else, truly understands our struggles. Our faith in Christ does not erase our innate emotions. Christ suffered comparably to any pain that we may bear. He understands our deepest emotions.

Intellectual Response

Job also responded intellectually. He knew the character of God: God is love. God doesn't just love (which leaves room for selectiveness of people and times to love); God is love. God loves all people all the time. With this knowledge of God, Job submitted to the circumstances, allowing God the choice of giving and taking. In contrast to his wife, who seemed to have momentarily lost confidence in God's redeeming qualities, Job trusted the fairness of God, and he expressed such to her. "But he said unto her, Thou speakest as one of the foolish women speaketh. What? shall we receive good at the hand of God, and shall we not receive evil? In all this did not Job sin with his lips" (Job 2:10).

Though we cannot always understand God, and we are sometimes unable to conclude any sense for suffering, we must learn to trust His will. God gives promises for every problem; He doesn't give explanations for every problem. At such times we must lean on what we know about God through His Word. We must trust basic qualities of God: love, mercy, grace, and truth. At crisis time we dare not reason regarding our worthiness of God's love. We do not earn His love; rather, His basic nature is to love us. He loves us when things are going well, and He loves us during the darkest trials of our lives. We need to believe that God never makes a mistake, and, therefore, we can always trust Him. To trust God is more significant than understanding why God allows disappointments to happen to us. Even if we know why a tragedy has befallen us, if we are to remain both mentally and spiritually healthy, we must still trust God for strength to endure.

Spiritual Response

Finally, Job responded spiritually: he worshipped. Job did not feel like worshipping and probably couldn't sense God's presence, but he still worshipped. He felt only hurt, pain, grief, and despair, but he still worshipped God. In a matter of hours Job's lifestyle completely changed. He went from extreme wealth to utter poverty. Fatherhood, fortune, and future were snatched in a single day. Still, he worshipped.

True worship is not a response to an emotional hype; it is recognition that God is God: the Giver, Sustainer, and Judge of all life. God deserves worship from His creation regardless of the circumstances. We worship Him because of who He is, not what the circumstances indicate. Worship is a choice. We can refuse to worship, withhold our love, and blame God for the tragedy. Such action doesn't change the past nor correct the present, and it may adversely altar the future God has planned. Worship doesn't necessarily change adverse circumstances, but worship sets us on a course in the right direction: God.

Suffering With Purpose

First responses are critical during the crisis moments, but the true test for most crisis situations comes in the long range of life. As Job's trials continued, his questions increased. He finally exploded with a series of questions: one hundred and eighty-one questions. I'm sure he felt his questions reasonable and worthy of God giving a rational answer, but Job soon found himself to be the student as God gave him a quiz. God doesn't always answer questions; rather, as in this case, in order to help Job see his place in the big picture of life, He asked Job a series of questions. Job found himself without sufficient answers to his personal questions to God, and he had insufficient answers to the additional questions God asked him. God's response to Job wasn't to minimize his significance in God's plan but to show God's proficiency in running the universe that He alone created, and He alone sustains. Job recanted, at least with his audible response.

> Then Job answered the LORD, and said, I know that thou canst do every thing, and that no thought can be withholden from thee. Who is he that hideth counsel without knowledge? therefore have I uttered that I understood not; things too wonderful for me, which I knew not. Hear, I beseech thee, and I will speak: I will demand of thee, and declare thou unto me. I have heard of thee by the hearing of the ear: but now mine eye seeth thee. Wherefore I abhor myself, and repent in dust and ashes.
>
> Job 42:1-6

Job found himself walking through a series of doors. Submission was a door that opened to a pathway toward acceptance; acceptance (without anger and bitterness) was the door toward a purposeful life beyond his darkest night. The same doors are available today. We can trust God's love as we walk through each door. And many times, if not most of the time, we must accept God's love without Him answering our "why" question. Jesus' question from the cross, "My God, my God, why hast thou forsaken me" (Luke 23:46) wasn't answered. Yet, His final statement, "Father, into thy hands I commend my spirit" (Matthew 27:51), a statement of submission, immediately opened a door into the next phase of God's plan for mankind's eternal redemption.

Jesus, when he had cried again with a loud voice, yielded up the ghost. And, behold, the veil of the temple was rent in twain from the top to the bottom; and the earth did quake, and the rocks rent; And the graves were opened; and many bodies of the saints which slept arose, And came out of the graves after his resurrection, and went into the holy city, and appeared unto many. Now when the centurion, and they that were with him, watching Jesus, saw the earthquake, and those things that were done, they feared greatly, saying, Truly this was the Son of God.

Matthew 27:51

While working as a pastoral counselor in a nursing home, I visited with a middle-aged lady who, in contrast to her severe medical condition, always seemed happy. A victim of multiple sclerosis at a relatively young age, her husband and children placed her in the nursing home for the constant care her condition required. She remained mostly immobile, totally dependent upon others for basic needs. She could neither roll over nor sit up on her own strength. During one of my visits I inquired of her recipe for such happiness. Her response included five points, which I copied down and carried in my wallet for years. Here is her formula:

1. Accept those things you cannot change.

2. Learn to enjoy the small things of life: a bird on the windowsill, a ray of sunshine spotlighting dancing dust particles, a glass of water from the hand of an aid.

3. Live one hour at a time, getting all you can from the single hour, for another is not promised.

4. Think and talk of the positive things in your life.

5. We have but one of two choices: to be happy or to be sad. Choose happiness.

Our problems aren't necessarily the problem. Too often the real problem is a result of our response to the problems of life. We may have limited control over circumstances, but we generally have control over our response to those circumstances. Happiness and sadness truly are personal choices. Over the last couple years I've had many occasions to observe Matt, a blind student who attends the Christian college where I teach. During the summer break he volunteered as a counselor at our church camp. He has reinforced my belief regarding choice. Whether walking the college hallways (stumbling over a crate someone thoughtlessly left), taking a classroom lecture (unable to see the overhead), or working with teens at camp (aware some take advantage of his impairment), he always seems happy. Why? Choice. He could be bitter, a recluse, or self-centered. Likewise, those are choices.

Job's response was multi-faceted. He responded to the immediate tragedy of loss of family and fortune by worshipping God and affirming his faith in God. He responded to the attitude of his wife by affirming that God is just. He responded to the accusations of his friends, defending his righteousness. He responded to his physical suffering. The intense and relentless pain elicited an emotional response that challenged his faith. Ultimately, he responded to God. This is where some refuse to venture for fear they will offend God. How do you tell God you are angry? Further, how do you tell God you are angry at Him? Elizabeth Landau shares interesting insight regarding expressing anger toward God: "If you're angry at your doctor, your boss, your relative or your spouse, you can probably sit down and have a productive conversation about it. God, on the other hand, is probably not available to chat.[3] Some are so angry with God they refuse to speak with Him. Their prayers diminish or cease altogether. From Job's example, God knows our thoughts, so it is meaningless to remain silent. Further, though God may not respond audibly, He hears our prayers. I believe, whether it's love or anger, we should verbalize our emotions to God.

Job's face-to-face encounter with God included a myriad of emotions, which are typical of what sufferers' today experience:

- The inability to feel God's presence: "Oh that I knew where I might find him! that I might come even to his seat!" (Job 23:3).

- The silence of God to his prayers: "I cry unto thee, and thou dost not hear me: I stand up, and thou regardest me not" (Job 30:20). The belief that God was testing him to see if he really loved Him: "But he knoweth the way that I take: when he hath tried me, I shall come forth as gold" (Job 23:10).

- A fear that his testimony of faithfulness was ineffective: "And now am I their song, yea, I am their byword. They abhor me, they flee far from me, and spare not to spit in my face" (Job 30:9-10).

- The condemnation from unrighteous neighbors: "Because he hath loosed my cord, and afflicted me, they have also let loose the bridle before me" (Job 30:11).

- A longing for the good days: "Oh that I were as in months past, as in the days when God preserved me" (Job 29:2).

Job affirmed that God was just and acquiesced that his friends were probably right: he had sinned. He suggested that God was withholding forgiveness and prolonging punishment for some reason he couldn't understand, and he wished God would tell him what to do so the pain would pass. His speech hinted of man's worthlessness before God and suggested God could just forget he ever existed. He seemed to entertain the "remove your finger from the bucket of water and watch what happens" philosophy. He bordered on cynicism and dabbled in fatalism. His feelings ran the emotional gamut.

> What is man, that thou shouldest magnify him? and that thou shouldest set thine heart upon him? And that thou shouldest visit him every morning, and try him every moment? How long wilt thou not depart from me, nor let me alone till I swallow down my spittle? I have sinned; what shall I do unto thee, O

> thou preserver of men? why hast thou set me as a mark against thee, so that I am a burden to myself? And why dost thou not pardon my transgression, and take away my iniquity? for now shall I sleep in the dust; and thou shalt seek me in the morning, but I shall not be.
>
> Job 7:17-21

Job felt trapped in a no win situation. He sought escape in his dialog with God. "I repent, so why not forgive me and stop the pain or else let me die?" Such an attitude challenges God's love for mortal man, which is in direct opposition to the nature of God. God remained silent, His silence probably His challenge of Job's thought process. Job's friends kept accusing him and demanding confession. Job argued if God would show him his error, he would change. He questioned why God was silent. He defended his status among his friends, challenging their wisdom. He experienced a plethora of emotions and lashed out in self-defense. He was a broken man, but like a cornered dog he fought on in desperation. Finally, God spoke with a voice so loud Job heard it over the roar of a tornado. A series of questions from God left Job speechless. "Moreover the LORD answered Job, and said, Shall he that contendeth with the Almighty instruct him? he that reproveth God, let him answer it" (Job 40:12).

Job realized to debate God was futile, and he says so. "Behold, I am vile; what shall I answer thee? I will lay mine hand upon my mouth. Once have I spoken; but I will not answer: yea, twice; but I will proceed no further" (Job 40:4-5). But in Job's heart he still challenged God's love and motives. God, who sees the heart, spoke again.

> Gird up thy loins now like a man: I will demand of thee, and declare thou unto me. Wilt thou also disannul my judgment? wilt thou condemn me, that thou mayest be righteous? Hast thou an arm like God? or canst thou thunder with a voice like him? Deck thyself now with majesty and excellency; and array thyself with glory and beauty. Cast abroad the rage of thy wrath: and behold every one that is proud, and abase him. Look on every one that is proud, and bring him low; and tread down the wicked in their

place. Hide them in the dust together; and bind their faces in secret. Then will I also confess unto thee that thine own right hand can save thee.

Job 40:7-14

At this point Job realized that, but for the grace of God, all mankind was doomed. He affirmed what he thought he believed before his suffering: God cares tremendously about a creation that doesn't deserve His love. He realized any righteousness he possessed was the righteousness of His Lord working through him. Perhaps for the first time in his life he saw himself in comparison to a holy God. "I have heard of thee by the hearing of the ear: but now mine eye seeth thee. Wherefore I abhor myself, and repent in dust and ashes" (Job 42:5-6). At this point Job totally submitted to the will and wisdom of God. The circumstances remained, but Job changed, and true repentance gripped his heart. He, not God, was on trial. No matter how absurd circumstances may seem, God is righteous in all His ways. Period. It was at this moment God started the process of changing Job's circumstances.

Points of Discussion

How may our responses to suffering be positive and negative? Right and wrong?

How may we determine if our emotional responses are acceptable?

Discuss both the Biblical and psychological principles regarding forgiveness.

Can happiness be acquired by choice? If yes, how can we choose happiness? If no, are some relegated to a life of sadness because of circumstances?

Is sadness always a sign of weakness or poor choice?

Chapter 7

The Response Of Friends

> When my father and my mother forsake me, then the LORD will take me up. I had fainted, unless I had believed to see the goodness of the LORD in the land of the living. Wait on the LORD: be of good courage, and he shall strengthen thine heart: wait, I say, on the LORD.
>
> Psalms 27:10, 13-14

News of Job's calamity traveled with the caravans. The reports stunned friends and business partners. Three of his friends sent a messenger to set up an appointment for a visit. This was mistake number one: a true friend would have come immediately. To give them the benefit of the doubt, perhaps they followed some type of cultural courtesy by their actions. Or perhaps their hesitancy was to coordinate their visit from afar, but from the dialog that followed, their visit seems more a corroboration, a spiritual conspiracy. From the report of Job's plight, their theology deduced an assumption before arrival. Groupthink tends to be safe. Three of your best friends agreeing as to the cause of your calamity can't be wrong. Job's friends drew a conclusion about him and visited to submit their supposition. What they found shocked them into silence, at least for a while. When they finally spoke, their words, like barbed arrows, pierced his heart and added pain to his wounded spirit.

This was their second mistake: they thought their chat would cure. Their "talking-cure" failed just as it still does today. Sufferers don't need our topper stories. To share our experience of pain doesn't minimize theirs. Such intended sympathy may come across insultingly. To say "I know just how you feel" is generally untrue. A story about our last year's surgery doesn't diminish their present pain. And please don't attempt to diagnose their symptoms with yours. You're not there to counsel or doctor them; you're there to show you care.

I recall an incident that happened in a Bible college classroom where I taught prospective ministers basic etiquette regarding ministry. One particular class consisted of a role-play where one of the students visited a grieving widow (a fellow student) at a funeral home (the front of our classroom). I assigned a young man the task of offering comfort while the other students observed and would later discuss his actions. He confidently walked to the front of the classroom where the supposed widow stood, her dead husband (a live student) stretched out on a table before her, and handed her a business card. Needless to say, we had a lot of discussion that day. To comfort others is to forget about yourself, your business, your interests, your victorious feats, and your battle scars. It is to focus on the need of the sufferer, without ulterior motives.

Job's friends committed a third misstate out of faulty theology. They adhered to a rigid belief that bad things happen because you've been a bad boy. As bad as things were for Job, he had to have committed some grave errors to receive such displeasure from God. They joined forces to convince Job of his obvious need to confess and repent of sin.

Job's friends heaped condemnation instead of offering comfort. No men have ever been more wrong about another. They judgmentally delved into the unknown cause instead of ministering to the obvious calamity. They had no idea Job was the poster child for God's confidence in His creation. Nor could they fathom the twists and turns this contest would take before God proclaimed to Satan, "See, my servant Job serves me out of love."

Job's friends had the privilege to assist in God's plan, but they forfeited their role by an insensitive spirit. If they had remained silent, they would have been of greater benefit to this suffering man. A drowning man doesn't need a swimming lesson; he needs a life preserver. Job didn't need a lesson about sin and confession;

he needed a shoulder to lean on, a tissue to cry in, an ear to listen, a hand to bind his wounds, and a heart to empathize. That would have brought repentance sooner than later. They knew the rules of God but not the heartbeat of God. "... not knowing that the goodness of God leadeth thee to repentance?" (Romans 2:4). The intentions of Job's friends may have been to comfort and encourage (they wept when they saw his horrible physical condition), but their seven days of silence was broken by words of condemnation. They unconsciously joined league with Satan as the antagonists of Job's soul. We can only assume their intentions. Perhaps they were afraid to interfere with what they assumed God was doing to Job. Their lack of attentiveness to his obvious needs seems indicative of a critical and judgmental spirit. "Judge not, that ye be not judged" (Matthew 7:1) seemed an alien message to them.

The theology of Job's friends represents the assumption of many: good things happen to the godly while bad things happening in one's life are indicative of personal sin, thus, God is punishing the wrongdoer. Repentance is the solution. Many perpetuate this defective theology, preaching the righteous will always be protected from problems while the unrighteous will always suffer because of their sins. Further, Job's friends assumed prosperity implies God's favor, while poverty implies His displeasure. The Bible teaches otherwise. A nineteenth century pastor, writer, prolific Bible student and teacher said it well: "Wealth is no mark of God's favor. Poverty is no mark of God's displeasure."[1] We must keep in mind the events of Job's life were pre-written Scripture. Job's friends, without the written Scripture, were still trying to figure out God and His ways of dealing with mankind. In their limited resources they arrived at some faulty assumptions about God. They falsely assumed, since Job had lost all, his sins must be many. However, one need only look at third-world countries, where Christians are constantly suffering, to understand the theology that "only-good-things-happen-to-good-people" is grossly flawed. The Bible doesn't teach the popular prosperity plan of many televangelists. Sadly, the prosperity teaching is often motivated by hefty budgets and excessive lifestyles. God's promises of blessing and protection were never intended to be a thermometer of spirituality. Those who live righteous (though offered many promises from the Lord) are never promised blanket exemption from life's tragedies. The opposite is true: "Yea, and all that will live godly in Christ Jesus shall suffer persecution" (II Timothy 3:12). We are promised exemption from eternal damnation, but even this is qualified with contingencies. No one will be dragged into heaven kicking and screaming and sinning.

The Biblical teaching that the righteous will ultimately prosper and the wicked will be defeated is true only when we include eternity. The writer of Hebrews, certainly inspired of the Holy Spirit, contradicts the "prosperity prophets" by pointing out that some of the Old Testament characters, who were heroes of faith, were anything but exempt from suffering.

> And others had trial of cruel mockings and scourgings, yea, moreover of bonds and imprisonment: They were stoned, they were sawn asunder, were tempted, were slain with the sword: they wandered about in sheepskins and goatskins; being destitute, afflicted, tormented; (Of whom the world was not worthy:) they wandered in deserts, and in mountains, and in dens and caves of the earth. And these all, having obtained a good report through faith, received not the promise: God having provided some better thing for us, that they without us should not be made perfect.
>
> Hebrews 11:36-40

Does this Scripture sound as if the righteous never suffer? Or consider the apostles, of whom history records only one, John, dying a natural death. Further, some say John had been dipped into boiling oil. His enemies sent him to the Island of Patmos as a religious prisoner of the Roman Empire. What a pathetic sight that must have been: an aged and French-fried apostle without a congregation! But on the Lord's Day we find him "in the spirit" and receiving revelation from Christ regarding the future of the church. Or, consider the life of Christ. "Looking unto Jesus the author and finisher of our faith; who for the joy that was set before him endured the cross, despising the shame, and is set down at the right hand of the throne of God" (Hebrews 12:2).

When Job's three friends came to visit they were unprepared for what they saw and heard.

> Now when Job's three friends heard of all this evil that was come upon him, they came every one from his own place; Eliphaz the Temanite, and Bildad the Shuhite, and Zophar the Naamathite: for they had made an appointment together to come to mourn with him and to comfort him (Job 2:11). After this opened Job his mouth, and cursed his day.
>
> Job 3:1

They found Job in despair both emotionally and physically. They listened as he spoke from a heart of anguish, doubt, frustration, and pain, but they didn't hear his heart-screams. They cringed as he scraped his sores with broken pottery. The painful procedure eased the pain from the boils that covered his body. They couldn't imagine the anguish of his spirit as he longed for the fellowship of his family, buried within eyeshot of the ash pile upon which he sat in contrition and mourning. Job's friends misinterpreted the situation as needing a theological explanation, and they attempted to offer one. With their finite understanding of God and life and Job's heart, they offered counsel.

Chapters three through thirty-seven of the book of Job record the dialogue of Job, his three friends, and a fourth young man who seems hesitant in challenging the wisdom of his elders. Their names are Eliphaz, Bildad, Zophar and Elihu. Though we can now scrutinize, it is not to condemn Job's friends; rather, it is to help us understand their theology lacked the essentials of God's amazing grace. Their actions also lacked basic neighborly kindness. Their words and actions seem heartless. Perhaps in studying the actions and attitudes of these who were notably wise, we may not be so offended when others repeat their failed attempts at comforting. Though family, friends, and neighbors try to help in our suffering, they often fail to say and do comforting things. It's an age-old problem. Likewise, we should refrain from offering such flawed theology to those around us who are suffering. Further, the horror stories about our personal illnesses and surgeries aren't necessarily as comforting as we sometimes suppose. No one needs our topper story to ease his or her pain.

It should be noted that the dialogues of Job and his friends, though recorded in Scripture, are not necessarily the correct way to handle suffering, nor are the remarks in their assumptions regarding God correct. Some of the insight of these men is true, but their actions and words were not recorded in Scripture because they were inspired of the Lord; rather, they were recorded because it is what they actually said and did to Job. Further, Job's response to his friends is not necessarily wise advice for us simply because the responses are recorded in Scripture; they are recorded in Scripture simply because they were the actual responses of Job regarding his suffering and the accusations of his friends.

We shouldn't be quick to judge Job, nor are we called of the Lord to judge others in their time of suffering. We are to comfort, encourage, help, and strengthen. We need not, as Job's friends erred, correct the emoting of someone in the throes of suffering. Job merely spoke out of the anguish and bitterness of a broken spirit and hurting body. Further, he'd lost hope that his soul was right with its maker. That deeply troubled him. It seemed obvious to him that his friends didn't have the correct answer, so he appealed directly to God. Those who suffer from great loss can certainly identify with his lengthy and anguished petition.

> Is there not an appointed time to man upon earth? are not his days also like the days of an hireling? As a servant earnestly desireth the shadow, and as an hireling looketh for the reward of his work: So am I made to possess months of vanity, and wearisome nights are appointed to me. When I lie down, I say, When shall I arise, and the night be gone? and I am full of tossings to and fro unto the dawning of the day. My flesh is clothed with worms and clods of dust; my skin is broken, and become loathsome. My days are swifter than a weaver's shuttle, and are spent without hope. O remember that my life is wind: mine eye shall no more see good. The eye of him that hath seen me shall see me no more: thine eyes are upon me, and I am not. As the cloud is consumed and vanisheth

Suffering With Purpose

away: so he that goeth down to the grave shall come up no more. He shall return no more to his house, neither shall his place know him any more. Therefore I will not refrain my mouth; I will speak in the anguish of my spirit; I will complain in the bitterness of my soul. Am I a sea, or a whale, that thou settest a watch over me? When I say, My bed shall comfort me, my couch shall ease my complaints; Then thou scarest me with dreams, and terrifiest me through visions: So that my soul chooseth strangling, and death rather than my life. I loathe it; I would not live alway: let me alone; for my days are vanity. What is man, that thou shouldest magnify him? and that thou shouldest set thine heart upon him? And that thou shouldest visit him every morning, and try him every moment? How long wilt thou not depart from me, nor let me alone till I swallow down my spittle? I have sinned; what shall I do unto thee, O thou preserver of men? why hast thou set me as a mark against thee, so that I am a burden to myself? And why dost thou not pardon my transgression, and take away my iniquity? for now shall I sleep in the dust; and thou shalt seek me in the morning, but I shall not be.
Job 7:1-21

Consider what Job suffered. I draw from the notes of author and editor Donald C. Stamps in his insightful outline on the anguish of Job's soul[2]:

1. Domestically: All his children were dead. He lost the camaraderie of his wife as she grieved for her children and perceived rejection from her God. There is no mention of any relatives coming to his aid, though they did visit when God reversed his tragedy (Job 42:11).

2. Physically: Job lost his wealth and his means of regaining such, since his servants, livestock, camels, and all means of commercial trade were

gone. He had none to care for his basic physical needs (Job needed daily physical care for his diseased body.) and perhaps no means for a physician.

3. Socially: Though viewed as an ancient Bill Gates, overnight, Job lost everything except his anguished wife and the few surviving servants who brought the tragic news. He experienced alienation from the community that previously rode the shirttails of his prosperity. His enemies seized the opportunity to mistreat him. A word of consolation from his three friends would have lightened his cross, but they added to the weight by their words of condemnation.

4. Spiritually: If ever there was a man who sought to serve God with his whole heart Job would have made the list. Now he felt God had not only abandoned him, but might well be punishing him for some wrong he knew not of. God's silence seemed an indictment.

5. Mentally: Job's intense grief, physical pain, loss of sleep, terrifying dreams, and sense of hopelessness pushed him to the brink of insanity.

6. Emotionally: Job experienced an emotional gauntlet of ambiguity, betrayal, fear, rejection, and despair. He sat upon an ash heap of hopelessness and considered death a relief.

Job's friends pointed an accusing finger and pleaded with him to repent. Eliphaz argued that the righteous do not receive such punishment from God. "Remember, I pray thee, who ever perished, being innocent? or where were the righteous cut off?" (Job 4:7).

Bildad picked up where Eliphaz left off, accusing Job's children of being sinful, thus the reason for their death. "If thy children have sinned against him, and he have cast them away for their transgression..." (Job 8:4).

Then Zophar attempts shock treatment by a matter-of-fact accusation that Job is a liar and is too proud to admit his errors. "Should thy lies make men hold their peace? and when thou mockest, shall no man make thee ashamed?" (Job 11:3).

The cliché "With friends like these, who needs enemies?" rings loud and clear in the Book of Job. And a fourth friend, Elihu, became the charismatic closer. After holding his peace, while Job and his three friends bantered, Elihu finally gave his summation of the situation and asserts that he's speaking for God. His attack doesn't seem as harsh regarding Job's sin; rather, he defends God's character and offers justification for anything God may have done to Job. His opinions are similar to Job's other friends, but he contends that God isn't as judgmental as mortals perceive Him regarding righteousness and unrighteousness. He concludes Job's real problem came about once he accused God. Thus the real issue is pride: Job's defense and accusation directed toward a perfect God positioned him on the wrong side of God. Though a bit ambiguous regarding how God views mortal man, Elihu believed Job had failed in some way, and God's punishment was a chastisement of love, not punishment, to evoke humility. If Job would acknowledge personal responsibility for his sin, God would forgive and bless his life again, and God's character (which Job had assailed) would be vindicated. Still, though somewhat veiled with a deep reverence for God's character, Elihu espoused the same faulty theology of his associates: good things happen to good people and bad things happen to bad people. If you're experiencing bad things happening to you, then you've been a bad boy. Job needed to repent and be good so God could do good things for him again.

> Behold, God is mighty, and despiseth not any: he is mighty in strength and wisdom. He preserveth not the life of the wicked: but giveth light to the poor. He withdraweth not his eyes from the righteous; but with kings are they on the throne; yea, he doth establish them for ever, and they are exalted. And if they be bound in fetters, and be holden in cords

of affliction; then he sheweth them their work, and their transgressions that they have exceeded. He openeth also their ear to discipline, and commandeth that they return from iniquity. If they obey and serve him, they shall spend their days in prosperity, and their years in pleasures. But if they obey not, they shall perish by the sword, and they shall die without knowledge.

Job 36:5-12

    These men were not Job's enemies; they were his closest friends. They were not mere acquaintances; they were his life-long buddies. They went to school together, worshipped together, and did business together. They knew him well, but they did not judge him well. Job needed a friend to support his faith in God; these friends found fault with his faith. He needed hope; they hurled into his face homilies that hurt. He needed to know that God still loved him; they reinforced his fears that God had left him. He needed assurance and affirmation; they made accusations and assumptions. And these were his friends.

    They didn't perceive what was taking place in the spirit world (nor did Job). Neither could they perceive that mortal man had the capacity to love God as Job loved God. Nor could they imagine God allowing such suffering of the righteous. Perhaps God was allowing them to glimpse Calvary, where Deity allowed humanity to suffer for the bigger cause: His love for mankind.

    Why do friends offer such hurtful statements? Without excusing such insensitivity, we can make some sense out of poor choices of words. Sometimes friends don't have a clue, but they're compelled by their friendship to say something. Some friends are endowed with an expressive nature that has to offer advice. Consider the Apostle Peter, Christ's selection to be the spokesman at the birth of the church. He wasn't afraid to speak up; still, he didn't know when to shut up. He made an absurd statement to Christ regarding the Bible incident referred to as the transfiguration. Mark, in his gospel, comments on Peter's comment: "For he wist not what to say; for they were sore afraid" (Mark 9:6).

Open-mouth-insert-foot disease isn't limited to casual conversation, nor to the unlearned. It's present in serious dialogue even among the scholarly. I've a friend whom I consider extremely knowledgeable who suffers from the absolute necessity to say something about everything. He's a critical thinker who's able to walk into a boardroom and sway a dozen freethinkers by his insightfulness and incredible ability to communicate. After he'd delivered a masterful sermon at the church I pastor, I handed him an envelope. Assuming it to be a check, he thanked me and said the usual "You didn't need to pay me. I'd do it for free." But he couldn't stop talking. He continued with "It's so kind of you. Some churches don't give enough honorarium to cover the cost of getting there." He proceeded by sharing horrid stories to support his statement. Somewhere deep into the conversation, he realized he hadn't a clue as to what the envelope contained: cash, a thank you card, a sizeable check, a small check. The look on his face said it all, but he couldn't stop talking. He tried to backtrack, to explain, and to apologize. I loved it.

Personalities are such that in seminars explaining the expressive nature and the natural inclination to talk, some participants will always vehemently disagree, fully disclosing their expressive temperament. Those gifted with communicative skills are often cursed with the previously mentioned foot-in-mouth-disease. Personalities that have to talk sometimes make ridiculous statements regarding suffering, for they are as confused as others about the why of suffering, but due to their nature they usually offer some explanation, right or wrong. Their analysis may be offensive and can evoke a counter-response from the one suffering. Already struggling to cope with the situation of suffering, the misunderstanding, insensitivity, and harsh theology of those who wish to help sometimes escalates the emotion. This seemed to be the case with Job and his friends.

How do we accept the intended meaningful words of friends who leave us hurting and angry? Foremost, realize the intention of the person is to be helpful. Though totally incorrect with advice, they care or else they would not visit.

So what is the sufferer to do when accused of harboring secret sin? Or how do you respond to the explanation that God has taken your child because He needs another flower in His rose garden? If not properly dealt with, insensitive comments may cause anger and resentment and destroy friendships. I believe it best to acknowledge true feelings. Repressed anger over a lengthy timeframe can resurface in harmful ways: disease, stomach disorders, and lingering bitterness. This doesn't mean we should speak angrily toward the offender; rather, we need to be honest about our feelings. We can disagree without attacking the one with whom we disagree.

Psychologists use the term response interval. This is the short time period between an act performed by someone else and our response to that act. During this brief period of mere seconds we can help or harm the situation. A good practice to avoid conflict is to filter our emotions through silent prayer, asking God for wisdom and patience in responding. The bitterness, hurt, and disappointment we feel will pass; however, unbridled responses may have lasting negative consequences.

Insensitive dialog can be viewed as poor judgment, not meaningful judgment. A few people are simply rude and purposefully make hurtful statements, but for the most part, their hurtful statements stem from poor judgment. Those endowed with an abundance of poor judgment need not receive our wrath. Furthermore, there are too few good theologians and spiritual comforters. Many simply operate from a selection of religious clichés they've heard, giving little thought to the rationale of the statement. For instance, "God must want another angel in heaven's choir, so he took your child" is offered as a comforting statement; however, the concept is irrational and lacks Biblical support. To the grieving parent such a statement makes God a selfish monster. Though such statements are meant to comfort, the speaker is a bit short on communication skills and has certainly not rationally analyzed the concept.

We are tempted to be angry at those who leave us frustrated by their comfortless conclusions about why some tragedy has befallen us. Such anger is wasted energy, energy needed to survive the storm of suffering. Forgiving and letting go can best correct some situations, often quicker than confronting the offender. How? Jesus established a principle regarding forgiveness. Just as there is a consequence for disobeying God's laws, there is a compensation for obeying.

And forgive us our debts, as we forgive our debtors. And lead us not into temptation, but deliver us from evil: For thine is the kingdom, and the power, and the glory, for ever. Amen. For if ye forgive men their trespasses, your heavenly Father will also forgive you: But if ye forgive not men their trespasses, neither will your Father forgive your trespasses.

Matthew 6:12-15

Christ's directive regarding forgiveness is that we forgive unconditionally, not because someone deserves or asks forgiveness. The Scripture instructs, "Forbearing one another, and forgiving one another, if any man have a quarrel against any: even as Christ forgave you, so also do ye" (Colossians 3:13). "Let all bitterness, and wrath, and anger, and clamour, and evil speaking, be put away from you, with all malice: And be ye kind one to another, tenderhearted, forgiving one another, even as God for Christ's sake hath forgiven you" (Ephesians 4:31-32). The wisdom of the Scripture is our Creator's operating manual for our lives. It is right, best, and safe.

By this time you're probably thinking, "But if I'm the one hurting, shouldn't the comforters be more considerate?" Theoretically, yes, but this section of the book is addressing the sufferer's reaction and not the comment of an insensitive comforter. Hopefully they're reading this book, realize their error, and will not repeat it. And maybe they'll apologize to you later, but probably not. These directives are written for the benefit of the one hurting. It's obvious that another needed book is *What Not To Say To Help Someone Suffer With Purpose*.

Brenda Goodman writes in Psychology Today, "If physical exercise had a mental equivalent, it would probably be the process of forgiveness. Researchers continue to tally the benefits of burying the hatchet—lower blood pressure and heart rate, less depression, a better immune system and a longer life, among others."[3] She references a case study of girls who had been sexually abused, and she explained that letting go of anger and the desire for revenge brought significant emotional and social improvement. However, she notes that attempts at reconciliation with the sex offender didn't bring the positive results as letting go of anger and the desire for revenge.

This is significant in that we sometimes misinterpret the meaning of forgiveness. To forgive doesn't mean the offender is guiltless, nor that what the offender did is excusable behavior. Forgiveness is not about the offender; it is about the person offended letting go of anger and the desire for revenge. You can forgive someone without a face-to-face encounter. Though Christ suggests we go to the one with whom we are upset and work toward reconciliation, I believe the Scripture isn't in contradiction with this case study: sexual sins are in a different classification than all others (I Corinthians 6:18).

Professional counselors suggest letting go of anger and the desire for revenge. Further, Christ's examples for us, and His instructions to us in the Bible, are clear: forgive; let it go; don't seek revenge; love.

Points of Discussion

Discuss the objective of calling or visiting with a friend who is suffering.

What are some of the Christian clichés we offer that may sound trite or insulting?

From a Biblical perspective what are some of the flaws of the prosperity message? How can we balance this message with, not only the realities of life, but with Biblical examples of those abundantly blessed of God with material possessions (Abraham) and those who had few material possessions (Paul)?

Discuss the six categories of Job's suffering and how we may relate.

Discuss the significance of the term "response interval" and how we may improve our response to those who insult with their comments.

Discuss the law of forgiveness as given by Christ (Matthew 6:12-15). What are some of the things you don't have to do in order to forgive?

Chapter 8

God's Response

> Cast thy burden upon the LORD, and he shall sustain thee: he shall never suffer the righteous to be moved.
>
> Psalms 55:22

Satan responded that Job would curse God if his suffering became severe enough. Job's three comforters accused him of hidden sin and argued that God was punishing him for such. A fourth friend, Elihu, though he didn't necessarily accuse Job of being punished for his sin, attacked Job about his attitude toward God's character. Instead of bearing up Job in his suffering, he took it upon himself to defend God's character and speak on God's behalf at the expense of Job's need for comfort.

With their task accomplished, Job's friends sunk into silence and waited.

The sky grew strangely dark greenish. Not a blade of grass twitched. A flock of birds sped radically past the five figures sitting upon the ash heap. Out of this awkward silence a tornado swept across the field. With no place to run for cover, the five men fell flat and clung to the ground. With a thunderous roar, the whirlwind hovered over them. Then God spoke.

God's response to Job and his friends begins in chapter thirty-eight of the Book of Job. In this age-old sagacious script, one lesson of extreme significance is God's silence doesn't mean His absence. From our advantage of having the written manuscript of this long ago event, we have insight to the situation that neither Job nor his friends had. We understand that Job is not just another person suffering from the consequences of mortality. God singled out Job for a spiritual purpose. God chose him for a witness against Satan. The events of Job's life serve as a textbook for all future sufferers.

After thirty-seven silent chapters, God literally and audibly spoke directly to Job. Ironically, He didn't address Job's suffering. He didn't give explanations for the suffering. Rather, God addressed the attitudes and the ignorance of Job and his four friends regarding Himself.

God's approach was a barrage of rapid-fire questions: questions to which Job had no clue as to the answer. This cross-examination consisted of a series of more than seventy questions about the wonders of creation, God's authority over nature, the animal kingdom, and the whereabouts of Job when God created the universe. Who? What? When? Where? Hast? Knowest? Canst? Wilt? Gavest? Doth? Shall? All these questions left Job and his friends open-mouthed. For once, mankind had no answer: neither the sufferer nor the comforters.

God questioned Job, "Who do you think you are to question my wisdom, my presence, my actions, my mercy, and my love?" God challenged Job to prepare for, not a physical battle, but a battle of wits. "You, the created, have challenged the Creator, and I accept the challenge. Stand on your feet like a man and prepare to do battle with the Almighty!"

God reminds Job of his created, and thus limited, humanity, while He, the Almighty, designed, created, and sustains not only the earth upon which Job lives but also the vast universe upon which the human can only gaze and wonder. God concludes, "If there is anything you know that I do not, speak up. Teach me." Then God became silent again.

Job attempts a meaningful response. "Then Job answered the LORD, and said, Behold, I am vile; what shall I answer thee? I will lay mine hand upon my mouth. Once have I spoken; but I will not answer: yea, twice; but I will proceed no further" (Job 40:3-5).

Job's response sounds right, but God challenged it. In retrospect we realize Job's words didn't elicit God's displeasure, for it was not what Job said that prompted God's response; rather, it was Job's thoughts. At this point the dialog took on another dimension.

Consider Job's paraphrased thoughts.

Suffering With Purpose

I understand, Lord. I am but small potatoes. I am out of my league. You win. I have opened my mouth in the presence of infinite wisdom. It was a mistake. I will say no more. My lips are sealed. I have a right to my opinions, but I will not verbalize them anymore. I have lived for you all these years, and I have tried to do right, but evidently you see it differently. I will not question your genius. You're the boss, and I'm the little guy. My bad. Chill.

Though God's questions silenced Job, he wasn't convinced in his heart he was wrong. Why should God bully mankind? Why use such intimidation? Why is He so callused to man's suffering? These seem to be Job's thoughts, but his lips remained sealed.

God's omniscience took the situation to a higher level. Job's silence hid nothing from God, who perceived the battle still raging in Job's heart, so God continued round two with more questions. The bottom line of God's second series of questions focused on mankind's eternal soul. Can mortals save themselves from their fallen and imperfect state? God expressed, "Then will I also confess unto thee that thine own right hand can save thee" (Job 40:14). To paraphrase, "If you could save yourself, I'd have no need to be in the picture, but you can't. Therefore, I'm here, not out of anger, nor as an autocratic despot, but as a loving creator redeeming his fallen creation from sin, from Satan, from self. No suffering you've endured can compare with eternal damnation. The eternal life I offer you justifies any amount of earthly suffering I may have allowed or sent." This is the summation of God's dialog. God's love for mankind, and the absolute necessity for sin's punishment, were ultimately carried out in the crucifixion. "For God so loved the world, that he gave his only begotten Son, that whosoever believeth in him should not perish, but have everlasting life" (John 3:16).

It dawned upon Job that God's priority in his life is not comfort. It is not healing, finances, nor position. God's ultimate concern is salvation for eternity. God asked, "Wilt thou also disannul my judgment? wilt thou condemn me, that thou mayest be righteous?" (Job 40:8). God's questions were designed to help Job identify his human imperfections. Clinging to self-righteousness as an argument against suffering not only revealed personal flaws, it accused God as unjust.

Job wore the garments of God's goodness so long he assumed they were of his own making. God's questions stripped him bare of his cloak of righteousness and left him exposed as he truly was apart from God's goodness toward him: "Behold, I was shapen in iniquity; and in sin did my mother conceive me" (Psalms 51:5). His contention of self-righteousness vanished. He had heard about God; now he experienced God. When he compared himself with God instead of others, he realized his own goodness was but dust and ashes compared to God's goodness. Job repented. His statement "I abhor myself" expressed his realization of his sinfulness when compared to the righteous Almighty. At fallen man's very best, he is still corrupt when compared to his Creator. Mankind in his fallen state is significant only because God loves him.

Job's story is a foretaste of Christ's suffering. Calvary reveals the awful penalty for sin and the abysmal state of mankind. Calvary happened not because we deserved mercy, but because God loved us so much that He, through the Incarnation, suffered in our stead for our sins. We, too, need to arrive at this conclusion: any amount of discomfort is justified that propels us to a destination of seeking God's righteousness. When we realize our fallen state of debauchery, we should fall at the foot of Calvary and repent.

In Job's early life God recognized his servant's heart. "And the LORD said unto Satan, Hast thou considered my servant Job, that there is none like him in the earth, a perfect and an upright man, one that feareth God, and escheweth evil?" (Job 1:8). We could say: "Satan, have you considered my servant, Job. One who, unlike you, chooses to serve me because he loves me?" Satan challenged God's evaluation of Job's self-motivated service to God:

> Then Satan answered the LORD, and said, Doth Job fear God for nought? Hast not thou made an hedge about him, and about his house, and about all that he hath on every side? thou hast blessed the work of his hands, and his substance is increased in the land. But put forth thine hand now, and touch all that he hath, and he will curse thee to thy face.
>
> Job 1:9-11

"He doesn't serve you with the heart of a servant," Satan challenged. "He's not submitted out of love. There's an angle to his pretense. He's of the seed of Adam, and deep down he's selfish and manipulating. He's motivated by hate and greed, not love. Stop being good to him and he'll not only stop serving you, he'll hate you."

God, who sees the heart, knew Job differently. He saw a true servant's heart: a creature loyal to his Creator. God trusted Job's innate ability to love Him instead of hate Him. In the end, after the severe trials, God specifically said to Job's friends: "...ye have not spoken of me the thing that is right, as my servant Job hath" (Job 42:7). Servanthood is the primary position from which God elevates us. It is the position unyoked by pride and unmoved by poverty. The servant's heart is unpresumptuous and unpretentious: only full of gratitude. It's the position Christ chose when living on the earth:

> Look not every man on his own things, but every man also on the things of others. Let this mind be in you, which was also in Christ Jesus: Who, being in the form of God, thought it not robbery to be equal with God: But made himself of no reputation, and took upon him the form of a servant, and was made in the likeness of men: And being found in fashion as a man, he humbled himself, and became obedient unto death, even the death of the cross. Wherefore God also hath highly exalted him, and given him a name which is above every name: That at the name of Jesus every knee should bow, of things in heaven, and things in earth, and things under the earth; And that every tongue should confess that Jesus Christ is Lord, to the glory of God the Father.
>
> Philippians 2:4-11

To follow Christ's example, we must acknowledge that God doesn't always give us answers to our perplexing problems; rather, He offers us, through His Word, assurance of His constant divine presence. Though much may be wrong with circumstances in our lives, all can be right in our relationship with God. We no longer challenge His love for us, though we don't understand why we suffer; indeed, we trust His divine wisdom for our lives. Though our prayers, like Job's, are sometimes tainted with anger, bitterness, confusion, doubt, and frustration, if we sincerely seek God, He will come to us. Not necessarily to change our circumstances but to give us grace to trust Him. The Apostle Paul of Scripture endured a long affliction from which he sought the Lord for deliverance but was denied. His example offers direction: "And he said unto me, My grace is sufficient for thee: for my strength is made perfect in weakness. Most gladly therefore will I rather glory in my infirmities, that the power of Christ may rest upon me" (II Corinthians 12:9). Paul learned that to endure affliction is to have the opportunity to have a greater fellowship with Christ.

Our greatest goal in suffering should not be an intellectual understanding of what is happening, but an awareness that God is present with us, and we can trust Him. No matter what the circumstances may be, He has not stopped loving us, and He is always sufficient for our needs. He is the Almighty God; nothing, nor anyone, supersedes Him. The King James Version of Scripture references God as the Almighty fifty-seven times. Of these fifty-seven, thirty-one are recorded in the Book of Job. This patriarch was chosen by the Lord to suffer unduly like no other Bible character; likewise, it was through suffering that he experienced God in a manner few humans are privileged to know: God the Almighty.

Job held a very special place with God. Satan refused to remain in a servant's role and vacated his seat of honor near God. Satan's prideful spirit caused him to lose his honored position. In contrast, Job, under severe persecution, maintained his role as servant. God gave to Job the seat of honor vacated by Satan. Perhaps Christ had Job in mind when he taught the people:

> Blessed are the poor in spirit: for theirs is the kingdom of heaven. Blessed are they that mourn: for they shall be comforted. Blessed are the meek: for they shall inherit the earth. Blessed are they which do hunger and thirst after righteousness: for they shall be filled. Blessed are the merciful: for they shall obtain mercy. Blessed are the pure in heart: for they shall see God. Blessed are the peacemakers: for they shall be called the children of God. Blessed are

> they which are persecuted for righteousness' sake: for theirs is the kingdom of heaven. Blessed are ye, when men shall revile you, and persecute you, and shall say all manner of evil against you falsely, for my sake. Rejoice, and be exceeding glad: for great is your reward in heaven: for so persecuted they the prophets which were before you.
>
> Matthew 5:3-12

James, the half brother of Christ, wrote to the suffering Jewish Christians scattered from their homeland in Jerusalem. His letter is perhaps the oldest of the New Testament books. It references Christ's Sermon on the Mount numerous times. In his letter, he doesn't mention he is the Lord's half brother; rather, he calls himself a servant. He expected no favoritism. In contrast, he explains that God's people aren't exempt from suffering. He reinforces the Biblical principle that suffering in this world by Christians is certain, but such suffering doesn't diminish their esteemed relationship with the Lord.

> Take, my brethren, the prophets, who have spoken in the name of the Lord, for an example of suffering affliction, and of patience. Behold, we count them happy which endure. Ye have heard of the patience of Job, and have seen the end of the Lord; that the Lord is very pitiful, and of tender mercy.
>
> James 5:10-11

Suffering is seldom a choice, but our response has options. "We count them happy which endure," James wrote. He well understood that serving Christ offered no exemption from suffering. The Jewish historian Josephus noted that James suffered martyrdom. Such an outcome is difficult for some Christians to comprehend and accept, but a host of examples in Scripture teach us that suffering should be expected and is beneficial. Why expect suffering? We are pilgrims and strangers journeying through a foreign land on a destination to our heavenly home. Adversaries abound. The land in which we sojourn is cursed. Diseases are rampant. We are foreigners and suspect.

What benefit can suffering offer? Suffering brings God alongside us. It drives us into His arms. We lose our desire for the earthly; we long for the heavenly. As our body aches because of the pain, our soul aches for His presence.

In the account of God's deliverance of Israel from Egyptian bondage, all desire for them to remain in Egypt was severed because of the devastation the ten plagues brought to the Egyptian Empire. There was nothing of significance to keep them in Egypt. Allegorically, when compared with the Exodus of Scripture, suffering is designed to drive the desire for Egypt from our hearts and replace it with a longing for the Promised Land.

Points of Discussion

Discuss an experience when you felt God remained far off. Why does God sometimes remain a silent observer?

Since God is omniscient, our silence has little significance, for He knows our deepest thoughts. Still, how far should we go in saying what we think and how we feel?

How does suffering find meaning in Calvary?

Discuss how God considered Job "...honest inside and out, a man of his word, who was totally devoted to God and hated evil with a passion,"[1] but when Job disputed with his friends by reflecting upon his personal goodness, God challenged him.

Discuss the concept of a servant's heart toward God.

Chapter 9

Helping Those Who Suffer

> And whether one member suffer, all the members suffer with it; or one member be honoured, all the members rejoice with it.
>
> I Corinthians 12:26

Job's friends didn't help during his suffering; furthermore, they added to his pain. They didn't administer the balm of compassion. On the contrary, their oratory seemed blasts of condemnation. Consequently, it's possible Job's distraction in defending against the attacks of his friends prolonged the healing process.

What if the three friends had truly tried to comfort Job? For instance, what direction might the Book of Job have taken if they had begun their speeches with, "We're not sure why all this has happened to you, Job, but you're our friend and we've come to stand with you, to pray with you, and to believe that God will somehow bring you through this?" But they did not. Instead, they theorized with their faulty theology, occasionally making correct observations, but frequently adding to Job's distress. For instance, Eliphaz enters into a discourse about a dream he had, assuming it was a vision from the Lord for this occasion. He built his theological case around a personal dream that Scripture doesn't affirm was from the Lord.

Job's friends failed to realize his vocalization of feelings was acknowledging his fears, not abandoning his faith. He spoke from a broken, confused, and hurting heart, not a blasphemous, calloused, or hardened heart. A crisis situation is not the time to determine who's at fault and for what reasons. It's not time to argue over whose end of the boat is sinking; it's time to secure the boat and head for the nearest shoreline.

A hurting individual doesn't need theology (a study about God). Hurting people need to see God in us, manifested by our compassion. In Christ's Good Samaritan story, it was faulty theology that caused the priest and the Levite to pass by the man beaten, robbed, and left to die along the treacherous Jericho Road. Their theology judged him as unworthy of their time and attention. Their theology—which consisted of a limited and distorted knowledge of God, mingled with traditions—justified limited compassion. They operated from the theology of Eliphaz, "Remember, I pray thee, who ever perished, being innocent? or where were the righteous cut off?" (Job 4:7). Consequently, they left the wounded man half dead, surely to die from exposure. The Good Samaritan didn't operate from a study about God; rather, he offered one of God's creation a helping hand. He never judged the man's worthiness, for he was too busy attending to his wounds.

Job's comforters failed. Their error is evident not only by the flaws we see, but also because the Lord rebuked them.

> And it was so, that after the Lord had spoken these words unto Job, the Lord said to Eliphaz the Temanite, My wrath is kindled against thee, and against thy two friends: for ye have not spoken of me the thing that is right, as my servant Job hath. Therefore take unto you now seven bullocks and seven rams, and go to my servant Job, and offer up for yourselves a burnt offering; and my servant Job shall pray for you: for him will I accept: lest I deal with you after your folly, in that ye have not spoken of me the thing which is right, like my servant Job.
>
> Job 42:7-8

Consider their errors:

- They were extremely judgmental.

- They didn't attempt to comfort; rather, after seven days of silence, they offered an immediate fix: repentance.

- Apparently they didn't pray with and for Job; instead, they pried into his life with their questions.

- They neglected compassion as they argued their theology: God blesses the righteous and punishes the wicked. Since Job was obviously being punished, he had to be wicked.

- They offered no help for his physical condition: no bandages, no medicine, and no tending to his wounds.

Remember the fourth person who visited Job? Interestingly, the Lord doesn't rebuke Elihu as sternly as He does the other three. Though younger than the others, he offered some positive insight into Job's suffering.

> Then was kindled the wrath of Elihu the son of Barachel the Buzite, of the kindred of Ram: against Job was his wrath kindled, because he justified himself rather than God. Also against his three friends was his wrath kindled, because they had found no answer, and yet had condemned Job.
>
> Job 32:2-3

However, Elihu's theology, too, was with error. Though he was on the right track in emphasizing that suffering could have a positive effect in our relationship with God, he still assumed Job had sinned. "Because there is wrath, beware lest he take thee away with his stroke: then a great ransom cannot deliver thee" (Job 36:18).

Elihu somewhat balanced the dialogue of Job's friends. He argued they condemned Job without proper answers. He challenged Job's self-righteous attitude, suggesting Job, because of self-perceived righteousness, expected better treatment from the hand of God. There are some positive qualities that Elihu manifested that are noteworthy.

- He was respectful of his elders. "And Elihu the son of Barachel the Buzite answered and said, I am young, and ye are very old; wherefore I was afraid, and durst not shew you mine opinion" (Job 32:6).

- He was a good listener. He waited in silence until the lengthy dialogue between Job and his friends had finished. Then, and only then, did he speak up. "So these three men ceased to answer Job, because he was righteous in his own eyes. When I had waited, (for they spake not, but stood still, and answered no more;)" (Job 32:1, 16).

- He was kind. Elihu used a phrase, "I pray thee," which was equivalent to "please." He acknowledged the wisdom of the others. "Furthermore Elihu answered and said, Hear my words, O ye wise men; and give ear unto me, ye that have knowledge" (Job 34:1-2).

- He did not choose to attack Job as the others had; rather, he tried to reason. "Now he hath not directed his words against me: neither will I answer him with your speeches" (Job 32:14).

- Elihu wasn't a backslapper, and he was honest: not brutally honest, just honest. "Let me not, I pray you, accept any man's person, neither let me give flattering titles unto man. For I know not to give flattering titles; in so doing my maker would soon take me away" (Job 32:21-22).

- He offered his words as an opinion rather than absolute fact. "Great men are not always wise: neither do the aged understand judgment. Therefore I said, Hearken to me; I also will shew mine opinion. I said, I will answer also my part, I also will shew mine opinion" (Job 32:9-10,17).

By considering the pros and cons of the manner in which Job's friends treated him, we can be helpful to someone in the clutches of suffering. We should consider the positive qualities of Elihu and make ourselves available to be used of the Lord. We can visit, send a card, or make a phone call. People suffering are not necessarily looking for theological answers; they simply want to know there is hope and there is someone who cares about them. James expressed it this way, "Pure religion and undefiled before God and the Father is this, To visit the fatherless and widows in their affliction, and to keep himself unspotted from the world" (James 1:27). James gives two principles as a mark of Christianity. First, look inward at motives and attitudes. To best help others, our relationship with Christ needs to be in order: pure and unspotted. Next, look outward: reach out in love to the suffering, allowing your life to be a conduit through which the love of Christ flows.

Our Lord makes quite clear His expectations when we deal with those who are suffering. Consider this paraphrase of Jesus' instruction on how He will someday judge our response toward those suffering and in need of our compassion. There are qualities Christ desires from us: a non-judgmental spirit, no ulterior motives, and impartiality. Consider this paraphrase of Christ's message regarding the final judgment:

> And the Lord set in judgment, and before him came all the people of the earth. And He divided the righteous from the wicked, according to the law of compassion. And to the righteous He proclaimed, "Come unto me and inherit the kingdom planned for you before the world was created. Come into my eternal peace, for when I was hungry, you fed me, and when I was thirsty, you gave me drink. I was without a home, but you took me into your own, and you gave me clothes from your own closet. When I was sick, you visited me in the hospital. And when I was arrested, you did not abandon me."
>
> To the wicked He pronounced, "Depart from me you workers of iniquity, into everlasting punishment, for when I was hungry and thirsty, you judged me as being a poor manager of money. When I was homeless and destitute, you accused me of being lazy. When I became ill, you rejected me, assuming that my sins had incurred the wrath of God."
>
> "But, Lord, we never saw you in any of those circumstances. These people were getting what they deserved. They received the judgment of God because of their undisciplined lifestyles and sinful ways, but

if we had seen you suffering, Lord, we would have come to your rescue."

Had not the Lord known their hearts and the true circumstances, they may have argued their way into heaven. But the Lord needed only to show them the faces of the suffering: the orphans, the poor, and the widows. It dawned on them they never turned a hand to help; instead, they had walked on by.[1]

Points of Discussion

How should we view the outbursts of emotions that come from those experiencing extreme suffering?

Discuss the errors of Job's friends as they ministered unto him. What could they have done differently to be more comforting?

Discuss the qualities Christ desires in us when dealing with others, particularly those suffering.

Discuss the author's paraphrase of Matthew 25:31-46. Can you see yourself in the picture? Do you like what you see?

Chapter 10

The Reward of the Suffering

> And if children, then heirs; heirs of God, and joint-heirs with Christ; if so be that we suffer with him, that we may be also glorified together. For I reckon that the sufferings of this present time are not worthy to be compared with the glory which shall be revealed in us.
>
> Romans 8:17-18

Job's relationship with God wasn't based on a fair-weather faith. His motive for serving God superseded material wealth. In the loss of health he clung to hope in God's goodness and mercy. Job's wife, after losing her children and observing her husband's awful condition, succumbed to a sense of hopelessness. She felt death to be a better alternative; consequently, she asked Job to curse God, probably assuming God would then let Job die. Job wouldn't consider such an alternative and proclaimed, "Though He slay me, yet will I trust in Him" (Job 13:15). We hear nothing more about Job's wife but assume she survived the tragedy. We read the conclusion of Job's life.

> So the Lord blessed the latter end of Job more than his beginning: for he had fourteen thousand sheep, and six thousand camels, and a thousand yoke of oxen, and a thousand she asses. He had also seven sons and three daughters. And he called the name of the first,

> Jemima; and the name of the second, Kezia; and the name of the third, Kerenhappuch. And in all the land were no women found so fair as the daughters of Job: and their father gave them inheritance among their brethren. After this lived Job an hundred and forty years, and saw his sons, and his sons' sons, even four generations. So Job died, being old and full of days.
>
> Job 42:12-17

We cannot fathom the tentacular reach of suffering. God's future blessings never erased the sorrow Job and his wife bore over the loss of his children. We aren't sure regarding any lingering conflict in their relationship. Remember the railroad track analogy: parallel tracks of blessings and pain, joy and sorrow? In the conclusion of the story of Job, we envision the track of blessing running alongside the track of pain. Job was blessed with children in his old age, but the glowing faces of his children at the breakfast table never diminished the memory of the gravestones silhouetting the hilltop at setting sun. This side of heaven we never escape the heartache of losing family and friends. A word of caution: the final chapter of Job's life may reinforce the misleading theology that God always blesses those who suffer for Him. Though this is generally true, it needs clarification. Consider, all suffering is not for the cause of Christ; some suffering is because of unfortunate tragedies and circumstances of life. Since God has not sent such suffering, He is not obligated to compensate blessing for distress. Further, God may never remove certain elements of suffering this side of eternity, but He always promises divine fellowship in suffering: "I will never leave thee, nor forsake thee" (Hebrews 13:5). God doesn't always choose to prevent suffering, even allowing death to consummate the process. The last verse in the Book of Job speaks volumes: "So Job died, being old and full of days" (Job 42:17). The cycle of earthly suffering continued as his family grieved over his death.

Suffering often seems senseless, and we can't explain all the "whys!" When we consider the Book of Job, we realize Job didn't have a clue to the background story. He wasn't aware of the meeting between God and Satan. The heavens never opened to reveal a cheering grandstand of angels nor God's smiling approval. Job only

Suffering With Purpose

saw and felt pain and sorrow, which he didn't understand, and God didn't explain.

I previously mentioned the New Testament writer, James, the Lord's half brother and leader in the Jerusalem church. He elaborates on Job's suffering to encourage those in the first century church to endure the persecution they were receiving because of their faith in Christ. He gives keen insight to the definition of faith, associating it with endurance. The word translated "patience" could better be understood as "endurance." "Behold, we count them happy which endure…" (James 5:11). James points out the end of Job's trial revealed the mercy of the Lord, but it never explained the reason for the trial itself. It's as if there's no end to suffering this side of heaven. James notes the bigger picture; he includes the life to come. "Be patient therefore, brethren, unto the coming of the Lord…" (James 5:7). The ultimate hope of the suffering of the righteous is not the end of the trial itself, for some trials seem indefinite. We are to keep our eyes upon the big picture: eternity. The finish line to which we look is the appearance of the Lord Himself to claim us for eternity! The patience, or endurance, which James spoke of doesn't guarantee deliverance from suffering in this world; it guarantees strength to endure earth's trials and ultimate deliverance in the world to come.

The writer of the New Testament book to the Hebrew Christians explains the dichotomy regarding individual suffering: the same faith that delivered some believers from suffering kept other believers through their suffering. Some are victors because of their faith; others are victims because of their faith.

> And what shall I more say? for the time would fail me to tell of Gedeon, and of Barak, and of Samson, and of Jephthae; of David also, and Samuel, and of the prophets: Who through faith subdued kingdoms, wrought righteousness, obtained promises, stopped the mouths of lions, Quenched the violence of fire, escaped the edge of the sword, out of weakness were made strong, waxed valiant in fight, turned to flight the armies of the aliens. Women received their dead raised to life again: and others were tortured, not accepting deliverance; that they might obtain a better

resurrection: And others had trial of cruel mockings and scourgings, yea, moreover of bonds and imprisonment: They were stoned, they were sawn asunder, were tempted, were slain with the sword: they wandered about in sheepskins and goatskins; being destitute, afflicted, tormented; (Of whom the world was not worthy:) they wandered in deserts, and in mountains, and in dens and caves of the earth. And these all, having obtained a good report through faith, received not the promise: God having provided some better thing for us, that they without us should not be made perfect.

Hebrews 11:32-40

The overall Judeo-Christian Biblical concept of faith significantly contrasts the "name-it-claim-it" mentality of some Christians. Here's a condensation of the numerous definitions and examples of Biblical faith into a four component explanation: faith believes in the existence of the one and only God revealed in the Scripture; faith has a genuine desire to please God and does so by following the directives of Scripture; faith encounters and accepts the grace God offers through the cross of Christ; faith endures unto the end. Conversely, we tend to translate faith into obtaining material things. In Hebrews chapter eleven, faith is about salvation, worship, finding the will of God, pleasing God, and enduring in spite of the surrounding circumstances; it has nothing to do with acquiring possessions. How can God be too entangled in the type car we drive or the new house we desire when most of the world doesn't own a car and lives in shacks? When God's interests are divided between people praying for their daily meal and those wanting a new Harley, it's no question as to who gets His attention. This statement is not to suggest God can't give us a new Harley; rather, it's to get us to consider there are more important issues associated with faith than obtaining something we don't really need (albeit God does seem to spoil us sometimes). Can you imagine King David of Scripture praying for a horse that was faster than his friend's horse so he could have bragging rights? Or what about Moses praying for God to give him a gold chariot just like Pharaoh's so he could ride in style? Maybe we're wasting our faith on frivolity. Shouldn't we use faith for the furtherance of God's Kingdom instead of more pleasure heaped upon self-interests? Shouldn't faith be more about relieving suffering of others—the needy and starving children of the world—instead of gaining more toys?

I've heard some exciting stories about faith associated with material things, but there always seems to be a backstory. Take for example my pastor friend who saved his money for an anniversary cruise but felt God speak to him about giving the money to a far more worthy cause.

> I had saved three thousand dollars to take a much-needed vacation/anniversary cruise to the Panama Canal area. I talked to a travel agent on Friday night, and we decided on the details; however, it was too late to make reservations until Monday morning. That Sunday an evangelist spoke on sacrifice. The Lord spoke to my heart, "You need to lead the way as the example in sacrifice and give your three thousand dollars cruise money to the building fund." And then He said, "Trust me."
>
> Well, I argued with the Lord about how much we needed a break, and it was for our anniversary. I said, "Lord, this really hurts." He replied, "That's why I call it sacrifice." I told my wife what I was about to do, and then I told the church what God had told me, not for personal recognition but to affirm the challenge of the evangelist was truly from the Lord. I wrote the check and handed it to the church secretary.
>
> I still hurt the next day, especially when I called the travel agent and told her the trip was off. By that Thursday, four days later, thirty-five hundred dollars came to me from unexpected sources. I called the travel agent back and got the trip scheduled. Not only did the church building fund get blessed, but the Lord also paid for our cruise. God is so good.[1]

After giving the money to his church, God miraculously provided him with the trip plus five hundred dollars for spending money. But this had nothing to do with God giving because my friend had faith to believe God was going to give back to him. It had to do with my friend caring more about the things of God than he did his personal desire for a needed break. And in this particular case, God evidently liked what He saw and rewarded it. But from a Biblical perspective I can't guarantee God will duplicate this for you because you have faith.

In contrast to God miraculously providing, here's my story of how God refused to provide a financial miracle. Years ago at a high-tech crusade promoting inter-city evangelism, I felt strongly impressed to give my savings to the cause. The only catch, it was money saved to pay my taxes. But faith said God would provide. I gave all. Tax day arrived, and my savings had not been replenished. I was embarrassed and, truth be told, a little disappointed in God. I had to face the taxman empty-handed. He worked out a payment schedule, but I had to pay the money from my weekly salary. Manna never fell from heaven.

My point? We can't manipulate God. There's no magical formula that makes God work a miracle on our behalf. God sometimes chooses to bless; in contrast, He sometimes chooses to watch as if from a distance. The "name-it-claim-it" philosophy errors in that it makes God "the one who pampers" instead of Jehovah Jireh: the God who provides. The "name-it-claim-it" mentality has deep flaws in parallel with Biblical faith. Some of the obvious flaws include:

- It makes you god and God your minion: God becomes a puppet (an impossibility).

- It's presented with the intensity of a multi-level marketing scheme, motivated by a host of testimonies of success. Peter's testimony of deliverance from prison is shared, while James' testimony of martyrdom is ignored.

- It's generally about greed, not need.

- It didn't work when Christians needed it most: when they were being fed to the lions.

- It's generally centered on you giving money to someone's pet project: you send him or her money and God will send back money to you.

- It ignores the backstories of perseverance and patience.

- It has an irrefutable defense: if you don't receive your miracle, it's because you don't have enough faith.

I hope I haven't discouraged you from asking God for a miracle. God is highly motivated by faith. He's extremely inspired by bold prayers. He is the "can do anything" God, except lie. I can share numerous examples of the miracles God has performed for my family, friends, parishioners, and me. I readily recall the time as a struggling pastor of a small congregation, my mother-in-law sent my wife five hundred dollars. At the time it was like a million dollars. It came at the close of a revival in which the income didn't meet the expenses. Yes, we reluctantly used the money to pay the evangelist: all five hundred dollars. And yes, after some time, God rewarded us with five thousand dollars, along with a reminder that it was for the five hundred we unselfishly gave to His work. Later it was a fifty thousand dollar blessing. We've never personally received a million dollar blessing, but we were a part of a million dollar miracle, so we know God can.

Though I have received manifold material blessings from the Lord, and rejoice at the myriad of testimonies of God's special favor on others, this book isn't about receiving more stuff. It's about suffering without God necessarily offering an explanation; it's about obtaining strength to endure in spite of the circumstances. The writer to the Hebrew Christians didn't ignore the multitude of those who received no miraculous relief from their suffering. Instead, he acknowledged their enduring pain and expressed that God's promise of relief from suffering goes beyond the limits of earth and this life. The assurance of ultimate relief from suffering surpasses our allotted time and human logic. In short, some sufferers must wait until Christ calls them home before they'll be relieved of their burden. Why? It's the curse of mortality. It's why Christ had to die. It's the one thing about humanity that needed fixed. It's the continuation of the saga of Job. It's the answer to Satan's argument that mankind serves God out of selfishness. "Have you considered my servant Job?" the Lord asked Satan. Some of you can insert your name in the place of Job's. You are among God's elite. You are special. Don't give up your distinctive status.

Have I discouraged you from praying for a better house or newer car? That wasn't my intention. In fact, I've never owned a house I didn't give credit to God for providing. It's okay—no, it's important—that you ask God for His blessing. And when the blessing happens, be sure to give Him praise. However, don't ever buy into the idea that blessings and spirituality are synonymous. And never use God and Scripture as a ploy to supply more toys. My neighbor told me a story about a friend of his who walked into a sports store to buy some equipment. His opening line to the clerk was, "Tell me what I need." The clerk responded (they were on a first name basis), "There's nothing in this store you need."[2] Jesus' instruction regarding prayer focused on our needs: God's will be done, deliverance from temptation, daily bread. Do we really need more stuff? There are too many Bible characters that walked close to God but received little material blessing, and there are too many wealthy heathens, for spirituality to be equated with stuff. Bless God when He gives special gifts; bless God if He does not.

Many promises of the Lord are fulfilled in this life. However, these promises may not be those tangible, calculable, houses and lands like Job received in the end. Rather, they may be the intangibles: peace, hope, joy, grace, direction, strength, and courage. These are priceless.

Points of Discussion

How might the final chapter of Job's life reinforce the faulty theology that good things always happen to godly people?

Discuss how Job and his wife enjoyed the blessing of their latter children while coping with the loss of their former family.

Discuss how those suffering may balance maintaining faith for a miracle while keeping focused on the big picture: eternity.

How do we avoid the trap of the name-it-claim-it mentality while maintaining faith in God's ability to provide a miracle?

Chapter 11

When Suffering Doesn't Make Sense

> My flesh and my heart faileth: but God is the strength of my heart, and my portion for ever.
>
> Psalm 73:26

In chapter one I mentioned a colleague who insisted that everyone must enter into a season of suffering. He explained that as a minister his hardships came early in life: his were the sacrifices of college days and some tough knocks getting started in ministry. When I first met him he was a veteran of suffering and seemed to have his hardships behind him. Shortly thereafter, a bout with encephalitis (an extended illness that almost killed him) was surely the peak of his suffering. Not true. I've watched him and his family through the last forty years and have realized those early years of suffering were only the tip of the iceberg. They were not tests that exempted him from future suffering; they were more like training exercises that equipped him for further suffering. The worst was yet to come. In retrospect, he, along with his wife and family, faithfully endured a tragedy that could have overwhelmed their confidence in Christ. Instead, their example is a testimony to God's sustaining grace through every trial of suffering. They graciously consented to share their personal story of a tragedy that still makes no sense. Here is their super-condensed version of some of the worst imaginable pain a family could endure.

On a crisp November day, we enthusiastically made preparations for an evening revival service. Our family had no idea how drastically our lives were about to change. After returning home from church, we received a call that something had happened to our beautiful, dedicated daughter-in-law, Carrie. Thinking it was a sickness or something of a minor nature, we went to her home, believing we could be helpful. This was not a situation that would soon come to an end. Carrie had been abducted in her driveway and brutally murdered. We were barely into the grief reaction of this terrible loss when we found ourselves suspects in the crime and embroiled in an investigation and trial that consumed our lives for the next several years.

Our son, a faithful Christian, was accused of this horrendous crime. The daily battle of proving his innocence compounded his personal pain of losing his wife, and this ordeal dragged on, seemingly, forever. We found that being innocent until proven guilty is a misnomer even in the United States of America. What a shock! Through those years of tests, trials, and loneliness, our lives were forever drastically changed.

We experienced that in times of great stress, trials, and sorrow, we sometimes feel alone and friendless. Many around us did not know what to say, or else they did not want to get involved. Others didn't understand what we were going through. Sadly, some passed judgment. During these times we learned to depend upon and communicate more and more with God. After all, His Word promises He will never leave us nor forsake us. Through our deepest trials we found this Scripture to be true. God knows, understands, and cares about all of our concerns, and He feels our hurts. We experienced that life is not always fair, but God is always fair, and He is always there. He grants strength for the day and comfort for the hour.

Often we believe that bad things do not happen to good people. How wrong we are! Job is a good example of this. Like Job we learned to praise God regardless. We recognized that God, though He doesn't need our praise, delights in our praise. We experienced that He takes pleasure in our trust in Him for all things. When we worship Him we focus on something bigger than our pain, and in so doing we take attention from ourselves. In the process Christ receives His rightful place in our lives and reigns on the throne room of our hearts. This attitude of worship sustained us through our years of trials.

Without the experience of personal suffering, we could not understand the feelings of others when they have similar situations. These trials give us a more powerful testimony of the goodness and greatness of God. Suffering does not always make sense to us, but God is always fair and always with us![1]

I observed firsthand the suffering of this dedicated Christian couple and their family as they endured years of uncertainty, loss, and change. They incurred an astronomical legal expense. Drained of necessary energy for their daily responsibilities of ministry, they resigned from the church from which they would have eventually retired, left family and friends to relocate in a distant state, and started over with life. After some time they accepted another successful pastorate. In retirement years their life is filled with purpose. They deeply care about people and remain involved in ministry. We speak often by phone. They aren't bitter about the past. Time has corrected some misunderstandings and has reinstated some friendships. They speak freely not only about their pain, which eludes earthly reason, but also about their present joy. In short, they remain wonderful people in spite of the horrible ordeal they endured.

My friends exemplify the words of the Apostle Paul when he described his ministry being filled with suffering. "We are troubled on every side, yet not distressed; we are perplexed, but not in despair;

Persecuted, but not forsaken; cast down, but not destroyed; Always bearing about in the body the dying of the Lord Jesus, that the life also of Jesus might be made manifest in our body" (II Corinthians 4:8-10). An evangelist friend preaches a sermon regarding this text. He calls the sermon "Living on the Right Side of the Comma."[2] He emphasizes the need to choose the proper side of the comma on which you focus. For Paul, the left side of the comma was overwhelming trouble; conversely, the right side of the comma was a refusal to be distressed.

I'm reminded again of the parallel train tracks. Though one is adverse to the other, they travel in the same direction. To abandon the track of suffering to avoid the difficulties of life also abandons the journey that leads us to our eternal home. It doesn't take a rocket scientist to interpret the analogy. Focus on the good things of life. Stay on track!

Points of Discussion

To remain Christ-like, how do you as the sufferer cope with those who abandon or pass judgment on you?

Discuss the concept of praising God in the midst of suffering.

If you are the one suffering, what might you do to help those who don't know what to do or say?

What are some of the things you should do in order to live on "the right side of the comma?"

Chapter 12

Daily Trust

> Let your conversation be without covetousness; and be content with such things as ye have: for he hath said, I will never leave thee, nor forsake thee.
>
> Hebrews 13:5

Life's calamities force some to live with daily uncertainty regarding future tragedy. The following account is the testimony of parishioners Bethany and Andrew Johnson, who live from day to day with an impending cloud of heartbreak looming above them. In situations like theirs, many turn to various coping mechanisms (good and bad). While some merely survive, a select few become testimonies of God's grace and strength. I have been blessed to observe firsthand some wonderful people whose exemplary faith in God's Word is both inspirational and instructional while enduring unbelievably painful circumstances. Bethany and Andrew are two such people. They agreed to share their story, trusting it will encourage others who are going through similar situations.

October 31, 2006, my husband, Andrew, and I eagerly awaited the birth of our first child, a daughter, Maci Raye-Lynn. My blood pressure elevated, and I was diagnosed with preeclampsia, which necessitated delivery sooner rather than later. Two days later I entered the hospital. The physician started me on two medications: one to induce labor and another to prevent me from seizing from my elevated blood pressure. Unfortunately, the attempt to induce labor wasn't working; the baby showed signs of distress. They decided on an emergency C-section. I remember being terrified. I can't imagine how Andrew must have felt. Off to the operating room we went. I am thankful Andrew was allowed to go with me, for this was the point that our lives changed forever.

When Maci was born, she didn't breathe for about thirty minutes. Andrew recalls seeing her little blue arm hanging lifeless as they attempted CPR. She was intubated, and they were able to get her stable enough to transfer her to a children's hospital. I was completely unconscious during this time. Andrew and his mom rode in the ambulance with Maci while my mom stayed with me. The pain of separation had begun. I had lost a lot of blood and was critical. Looking back I cannot imagine how terrified Andrew must have been; it breaks my heart that he had to go through such emotional trauma without me. Once he got Maci settled in at the neonatal intensive care unit, he left his mother to look after her and returned to be with me. Though it broke his heart to leave Maci, he wanted to check on me.

I had been sedated since the surgery while my blood pressure returned to normal; so, it was two days later they told me what had happened. It was on the third day my doctor agreed to release me on a day pass to go to the other hospital to see my daughter for the first time. It seemed so surreal to me when I saw her. For nine months I bonded with her in the womb, felt her movement, and envisioned my life with her. How could this be my child lying there lifeless? I held her and nervously waited to speak to her doctors. I stayed with her as long as I could physically endure, for the pain from surgery and weakness from loss of blood were exhausting. The next day I went again to see my precious daughter. Our entire family gathered to meet with the neurologist. He told us he had done numerous scans of Maci's brain, and the brain activity was minimal to none. He explained our child was deprived of oxygen too long, and she was brain dead. He told us we needed to decide whether to keep her on life support.

Andrew and I were both twenty-two years old, and we had to make this huge decision. It is the hardest decision we have ever made. We discussed the dilemma at length with our parents and decided it best for Maci if we allowed the ventilator to be removed. Seconds after making that decision, the nurse rushed in to let us know things were looking worse, and we should come quickly if we wanted to be there when Maci passed away. I went to her, and with Andrew by my side, I cradled her little body. Her oxygen level dropped, but then it went back to normal ranges. As I held her I prayed to God, "Lord, please don't make me make this decision." With tears streaming down my face, I prayed for the Lord to take her to heaven without us having to decide to end her life.

After hours of waiting and watching, I couldn't take it anymore. Andrew and I decided we would let them turn off the life support, but we could not stay to watch. This is a decision I regret. If I had it to do over again, I would not have left her, but I can honestly say I did the best I could at the time, and God has given me peace about our leaving her. Our parents agreed to stay with her until she took her last breath.

When Andrew and I left the hospital, I believed with my whole heart that the Lord would do a miracle, and they would call and tell us she had started breathing on her own when they turned off the ventilator. This did not happen. The next morning I woke to realization that no call had been missed on our cell phone. Maci had not been healed, and she was indeed gone. She had lived only five days. How was I going to go on without her?

Maci passed away early on Wednesday morning, the same day as our midweek church service. Andrew and I decided we were going to church that night. I felt so alone and empty, and the only place I knew to go was to the church. I believe two things happened the moment we decided to attend church that night. First, the Lord changed the message the evangelist planned to preach. Second, the devil tried to prevent us from being there to hear the sermon God prepared just for us. Several obstacles got in our way; however, we were determined to attend church. Please realize we didn't go to show off our strong faith; conversely, we went because we literally didn't know what else to do. I stepped inside the church sanctuary and immediately broke down sobbing. I was broken to my very core. Our hearts were shattered. The loving church family gathered and prayed for us, but it wasn't until after the sermon that Andrew and I received our first steps of healing from the Lord. The evangelist specifically prayed for us, and I still recall the words he spoke to God on our behalf. "Lord, give them peace from their heads to their feet, peace that surpasses all understanding, God. Give them the peace that you have given me in the loss of my father." His compassionate prayer came from personal loss. At that moment God's peace flooded my heart. It felt like something swept over me from my head to my feet. I could feel a heavy weight being lifted. It wasn't that I didn't feel sadness for the loss of my daughter; rather, it was that I didn't feel hopeless or overwhelmed anymore. Thankfully, Andrew experienced the same. God is so good!

I won't tell you we haven't struggled since that experience, but I will tell you it has never been as intense as it was before that moment. It has taken us years to get to the place we are today. There have been good days and bad. Maci would have been five years old now, and we still miss her every day, but we find hope in the fact that one day we will see her again.

In hindsight I now see that God prepared us for the trials that were ahead. I had no idea we would face the circumstances we have since Maci's death, but because of the relationship we built with Christ during that trial, we are able to face our problems today. It is true that the Lord draws us close to him in our valleys of life because of the looming and treacherous mountains ahead.

It was August of 2007 as Andrew and I planned a wedding anniversary trip to Gatlinburg, Tennessee, that I found out I was pregnant with our second child. I could not have been more excited. I longed so much for a child that my heart literally ached. Off we went to Tennessee with so much excitement and anticipation we couldn't wipe the smiles off our faces. When we returned home I made an appointment with an obstetrician. Because of all the problems I had in my pregnancy with Maci he wanted to do an early ultrasound. I was about eight weeks along when I went for the ultrasound. The technician explained the baby appeared to have some fluid on the back of the neck. My heart sank. I could not believe this was happening. She couldn't give me any details but said it could be a sign the baby had Down syndrome. I went home and broke the news to Andrew. I made an appointment with the recommended specialist and went for a second ultrasound. Andrew was unable to miss work; so, my mom and mother-in-law went with me. The second ultrasound confirmed a huge sack of fluid on the back of my sweet baby's head. The doctor explained our baby had a cystic hygroma. She seemed very surprised I had not miscarried. She told me to make a follow-up appointment, but she really didn't think I would have a need to return because she assumed I would miscarry. I came home and told Andrew the news with fear shaking my voice.

I went for another appointment with my original obstetrician who recommended I see a different specialist. Unhappily, I made the appointment and went home. At church that Wednesday I went forward for prayer. I cried out to the Lord with a desperation I had never had before. I didn't care who heard me or what anyone thought of me. I was, like Hannah of the Bible, desperate for the Lord to intervene. The next week I went to the new specialist, but with his 4D ultrasound machine, he could not find a cystic hygroma. I knew God heard the cry of a heartbroken mother and healed my baby of the cystic hygroma that, at best, would have terribly disfigured him. We carried on cautiously with my pregnancy, visiting the doctor every week for most of the nine months. On April 2, 2008, Landon Robert Johnson was born. We loved him more than life.

More bad news awaited us. I was in the recovery room resting from my repeat C-section, when Andrew came in to tell me they could not get him to latch on to a bottle because of a cleft palate; so, they were going to give him a feeding tube. I remember asking, "Is he breathing on his own?" Andrew answered, "Yes," and I said, "Then I don't care as long as he is fine." The cleft palate in the soft part of his mouth was not visible from the outside, but Landon would require surgery to repair it when he was older. I was unaware this was a glimpse into the unfamiliar world we would soon come to know.

We excitedly took Landon home and relished four months of bliss. At his four-month check-up, our world began tumbling again. The pediatrician expressed concern that Landon was not meeting his developmental milestones. His limbs were floppy, and that concerned the doctor that something more serious might be wrong. We saw a host of specialists, trying to determine if something was wrong. When Landon was six months old, the genetic test came back. They determined he had a condition called Werdnig-Hoffman disease, or Spinal Muscular Atrophy type 1, as they now call it (SMA 1). We were given the devastating statistic that SMA is the number one genetic killer in children under the age of two. Our pediatrician gave us no hope. He told us with absolute certainty Landon would not see his second birthday. We were told to take him home and love him for how ever long we had him. Thankfully, the genetics specialists were open to looking for other hospitals that had experience with this disease, and they referred us to Dr. Brenda Wong in Cincinnati, Ohio. We live only two hours away, which may seem like a long distance to some, but we have befriended people who drive ten and twelve hours to see these doctors. When we met Dr. Wong, she overwhelmed us with information. Less than one week after we were told our child had this horrible disease, we were putting him through multiple tests to determine the machines he needed just to stay alive.

It seemed once again our lives were spiraling out of control. We were scared and wondering where God was in all of this. Why would Jesus heal this baby of one thing only to let him suffer another? I don't know why God allowed this to happen, but we have realized through the past four years that He has a plan! We have been in the pediatric intensive care unit more times than I would care to remember. After the first week in the hospital, things were looking worse rather than better. Our longest stay was ten weeks straight.

When my father-in-law stopped at the church, our pastor's wife and fellow parishioners prayed with him. During that prayer time the Holy Spirit gave us a unique message that said, "I know your storm is raging, but I am with you in the boat. I am in control." Wow! I can't tell you how many times over the past few years, in the midst of illness and fear, I have thought back on that message and found strength.

Now we are approaching Landon's fourth birthday! Andrew and I are amazed at how much he has accomplished. If you just look at what he can't do, you see a child who can't move, can't speak, can't swallow, can't eat, can't cough, and can't run. He can't do most things a normal child his age does; however, he is the happiest child I have ever met. He can't speak, but he can communicate his wants and needs. He can't run around, but he smiles every day and lights our world when he does. He loves when Andrew straps him onto a gurney attached to a bicycle and takes him for neighborhood rides. His eyes can tell a story in just one look. This week he started pre-school and loves it.

God is teaching us through Landon to appreciate the little things in life. He is teaching us to appreciate every day. When I look at Landon my heart fills with so much love I can barely contain it. I realize that even though he is not perfect by the world's standards, I would not love him one bit more if God completely healed him. I think about God's love for me, and if I love Landon this much, how much more must the Lord love me? He has never abandoned us in these trials, and just when we needed it most, He sends us a sign that He is with us. He has carried us through very dark places and given us strength to stay together. The things we have been through are hard on a marriage, and even though there have been good times and bad, God has given me a husband who stands by me through it all.

Through Landon's disease we have been able to meet some wonderful people. It is our prayer that

God will use us to bring them to truth and salvation. Whatever His purpose is for us to walk this road, we want to be used for His glory.

I have watched my child melt the hearts of medical staff with just a smile. He is more precious than I could ever say, and we are blessed to be his parents. My prayer is that the Lord will heal Landon completely, and he will be with us until the Lord comes back. I don't know what the future holds for our family, but I know what is in our past. The Lord got us through all of that; so, I know He will never leave us alone. He will bring us through whatever the future holds.[1]

Points of Discussion

Discuss how you gain strength to endure the agony of watching a child suffer or die.

Though you may desire quiet or aloneness as you cope with loss, what are the reasons for attending church?

How do you keep from abandoning faith to pray when God does not answer your most heartfelt prayer?

What are some of the disciplines needed to cope with the stress of living day-to-day knowing impending disaster lurks in the shadows?

Chapter 13

When The Pain Won't Stop

> Looking unto Jesus the author and finisher of our faith; who for the joy that was set before him endured the cross, despising the shame, and is set down at the right hand of the throne of God.
>
> Hebrews 12:2

I recognized uniqueness about Thomas Marek from the first day I met him. Over time his story unfolded: unbelievable pain grips his body continually. Here's his story and how he learned to endure the daily suffering that does not stop.

> They say a journey starts with a single step, though my step seemed just like the one before it. I never knew I would make the front page of the newspaper, but I managed to do so with a little help from someone else (not in the manner that I would have chosen). I traveled a particular state highway many times, but only God knew this was where I was going to start my incredible journey of pain. From a concealed side road, a young woman ran a stop sign and broadsided my one-ton truck. The speed and power of her older Buick folded my truck in half and sent it spinning sideways along the highway. After flipping a few times, it came to rest on its roof. First responders cringed, for they knew this was a fatal

accident. Little did they know, and I now realize, God had other plans.

A day turned into weeks, weeks into months, and months into years. The years have become decades, and still the journey of pain continues. After many surgeries and surgical procedures, with months of physical therapy and more than four hundred doctor visits, I no longer count. I manage to make it day by day.

PAIN. What is the hardest part of pain? Most assume the obvious: the pain. If you listen closely to the words of a chronic sufferer, you hear something else: the pain of a lost identity. Senior citizens tell stories of their past: the things they used to do. They share their accolades of yesterday, but if you listen closely, you hear something more. You hear how time, age, and ailments have taken their toll and how they can no longer do the glorious feats of yesterday. They have lost their personal identity. This emotion is also true regarding those experiencing constant pain.

Imagine going to bed on your thirty-ninth birthday and waking up to find the number of your years has been inverted. You are now ninety-three instead of thirty-nine. Your first response is disbelief, the first of several stages. You run to the doctor and try to get some kind of grip on the moment, something that makes sense of what is going on, but the more you look to find the answer, the more it slips through your fingers. After much disappointment you enter the frustration stage. At this point of your life, there is no answer to what is happening. No matter where you look or how hard you try to put a handle on what is left of your life, there are no words that seem to fit. When you have exhausted the frustration stage, the door to anger opens. Many pitch their tents here and set up permanent housekeeping. Here is the unconquered hill on which some die. With denial

Suffering With Purpose

and frustration as roommates, it becomes easy to live in this third world of anger. You don't know who or what to be angry at. The doctors? The affliction? Life? Spouse? God? Okay, I'm angry at all of the above. I can be angry at everything, everyone, all the time. But to do so will not make me better, and it will not turn back the clock so I am thirty-nine again. There has to be a better answer to this dilemma than anger.

Consider this scenario: If you woke up and found a telephone pole had fallen on top of your car, would it help to be angry at the pole? No. Would it help to yell at it, beat it with a chain, or throw something at it? No. So why waste good energy on the pole? Remember, you are now a ninety-three year old body. Since beating the naughty pole for falling on your car would only cause you more pain, the best thing to do is not allow the negative thoughts to control the moment. No, it's not easy, but the one thing you have control of is staying calm and reacting positively to the situation that has just presented itself to you. A sigh is good, for it relieves the pent up frustration, allows you to better assess the moment, and works for solving the catastrophe of the here and now. What about the pole? Call the insurance company, turn in a claim, and give your problem away. You now find that what looked to be bad at the moment turned out to be a newer, better, lower mileage car. If you look for the bad, you will find it. If you look for the good in a situation, when the smoke clears, you may find a sparkling diamond hidden in the grass.

The elderly's reminiscence of the accolades of yesterday creates a shield against self-incrimination and doubts of self-worth. They attempt to explain why yesterday they could, but today they cannot, all the while without a visible wound to hang their hat on. Since we tend to judge each other by the law of the jungle, our self-worth is hinged to what we are able to kill and drag back to the camp. But a thirty-nine year old person in chronic pain cannot perform any more than the senior citizen. The body revolts, unable to function, as if you are ninety-three. No matter how hard you want to produce, you are unable to close the big deal or acquire the huge bonus that allows you to supply the needs of your family and have a surplus to help others. You are faced with reality that without Divine intervention this chapter of life is over. It is easy to become and remain angry.

Once through these stages we enter what I call the Dead Zone. This stage is different than the others because here the emotions are dulled. Some slip into a world of depression, where all the meds in the world can't remove the lingering loneliness. It's like living in a fish bowl, perceiving everything going on in the outside but unable to participate. It's like watching yourself in a drama, yet not feeling what your audience is feeling, nor able to interact in the script. In the Dead Zone you feel numb.

You have got to escape the Dead Zone, but how? Here is where the human ability to choose can be your greatest asset or your worst enemy. Do you stay here for the rest of your life, accept what is happening, and make it your pet snake? Or do you fight against what has happened? With desperation to leave the Dead Zone and feel again, you may consider many things you would never have considered prior to your affliction. The unspeakable are played out within the mind. Like a prisoner you plan your escape. Or like the ship in a bottle longing to be set free, to feel the wind in your sails, and to ride the waves once more, you plan and scheme mentally. The battleground is the mind, and the enemy is the tantalizing temptations of the flesh. Suicide could end all the pain. A stolen bottle of meds could suffice. Self-pity renders you rubbish. Why not die and decrease the surplus population? Or in the words of a little girl whose mother flushed her dead goldfish down the toilet, and later, when the little girl caught the flu, she said, "Mom, just flush me down the potty with the fishes." But this is not the answer. Then what is the answer? Is it spiritual inspirations such as hope and faith? This is not as easy as some may think, for these seem to have died when you entered the Dead Zone. How do you bring life back to the dead? You must decide to live again.

Are faith and hope really dead? No, they are not dead, but they are transformed as you have been. And we have now compounded the pain of our affliction by doubting God. This combination does not make one feel extremely victorious. But we are encouraged to know that Abraham of the Scripture doubted God and yet was deemed the "Father of the Faithful."

Fighting the Dead Zone

The Scripture explains," For as he thinketh in his heart, so is he..." (Proverbs 23:7). Further, the definition of faith and hope are connected to our thought process: "Now faith is the substance of things hoped for, the evidence of things not seen" (Hebrews 11:1). Faith and hope are somewhat like a dream. I can still dream in the Dead Zone, and the wonderful thing about this is I can control what I dream. The Dead Zone has no power over my ability to think and dream, and if I still have these, then I still have faith and hope. With these the impossible vanishes.

The Power of Thought

In the mythical story of Peter Pan, the thing that made him soar above his adversaries was his "happy thoughts." This concept was true long before film and is Biblicaly based: "Finally, brethren, whatsoever things are true, whatsoever things are honest, whatsoever things are just, whatsoever things are pure, whatsoever things are lovely, whatsoever things are of good report; if there be any virtue, and if there be any praise, think on these things" (Philippians 4:8). We must find our own "happy thoughts" to fly above this corporeal body. Thoughts turn into actions and actions into consequences. Knowing we have control of our thoughts, we need to think purposeful thoughts. Purposeful thoughts bring fulfillment to your life.

The Bible indicates a special purpose for the afflicted by James' question, "Is any among you afflicted?" He then gives direction to the afflicted: "Let him pray." When we grasp this concept, we move beyond the Dead Zone and into purpose, for our prayer is not just about us, about our affliction; it can be for others. Our prayer can be with greater compassion and fervency, for we know how the afflicted feel. We can better fulfill the ministry of Christ: "The Spirit of the Lord is upon me, because he hath anointed me to preach the gospel to the poor; he hath sent me to heal the brokenhearted, to preach deliverance to the captives, and recovering of sight to the blind, to set at liberty them that are bruised" (Luke 4:18). The army of the afflicted can better minister to the afflicted of this world, a number without end and growing exponentially. But to minister to others, one must first gain control of personal thoughts.

Now in the Moment

When dealing with pain, it is easy to focus on the past and project the pain into the future. This produces anxiety in the present. But in actuality, all we should consider is the present. We have no control over what happened at eight in the morning, and we may dread the approach of the night with a negative contemplation of what is yet to come. This is futile regarding pain, for we cannot control the past or the future. The present is all we have left. So how is this moment? To control the present we must focus on happy thoughts: the marvel of nature, the varied colors and shapes of the clouds, and the smells of the air. We can focus on the positive of the moment; everything else is mere clutter, crowding our moment. We must seize the moment and the positive surroundings it affords rather than allow the moment and the pain to seize us.

How do you grab the moment when the moment is filled with so much pain? Let me explain from my personal pain, which comes with the natural process of simply breathing. There are days I must control the mind to endure the unbelievable pain that comes with each breath. My pain comes in waves, like a destructive wind causing tree limbs to whip and lash like a whip to the back. At that moment, when the limbs are about to rip into my flesh, I breathe slowly and deeply, imagining my entire body being air itself. With this imagery the pain passes through my airy body without its evil talons ripping into my flesh. It may sound like a child's game of make believe, but this mental exercise has the ability to get me through the intense moments when, otherwise, all I feel is pain. There are various ways to own a moment; so, find what works for you and use it.

Via Dolorosa: The Way of Suffering

I have learned to endure by taking one moment at a time and claiming promises of Scripture such as: "For we know that if our earthly house of this tabernacle were dissolved, we have a building of God, an house not made with hands, eternal in the heavens" (II Corinthians 5:1). The old hymn says it well: This world is not my home. As I travel this road of pain (not by choice), I hear fellow pilgrims express the positive side of suffering, sometimes the exact words: "I don't like the pain, but I am grateful, for it has opened to me a new world of compassion and sensitivity that I never knew existed."

An instantaneous miracle would be wonderful. I seek and believe for my instantaneous healing, but if God chooses to heal me slowly, as an open wound heals, I will accept that. But if no healing occurs, I am still full of hope, for this I know; "...this mortal must put on immortality" (I Corinthians 15:53). This earthly existence is only for a moment in time, not for eternity. Our destiny is heaven; no matter the road God leads us down. Some of us are enduring the road of suffering, but there is a final and victorious stage on the road of suffering. So, for my journey, to God be the Glory![1]

Points of Discussion

Discuss how constant pain becomes secondary to loss of identity.

How do you advance through the stages without becoming stuck? Are these emotions evidence you are an unspiritual person?

Why is suicide never the answer?

How do you resurrect from the Dead Zone?

Discuss the concept of the blessing of pain.

Chapter 14

What I Have Learned

> Not that I speak in respect of want: for I have learned, in whatsoever state I am, therewith to be content.
>
> Philippians 4:11

Early in this book I mentioned my wife, Nancy, and talked somewhat about her physical suffering. Her situation reminds me of the widow lady in Scripture who spent all the money she had but grew worse. For three years we have journeyed that road. We're grateful to have found physicians who diagnosed her illness and have been encouragers along the journey, but the cure has been more elusive. An avid writer, due to the constant and intense pain, she was unable to journal. It's thrilling after these many months to see her journaling again. Here are some of her thoughts regarding her suffering:

> Paul Ciholas, in his excellent book Consider My Servant Job states, "Faith is what remains when we lose everything."[1] When everything else was gone, Job's faith stated, "Though He slay me, yet will I trust Him." His faith accepted that his adversities came from his Creator. Nowhere does he give the devil credit for any of his problems. Basically he was saying, "I am suffering at the hands of God." That is strong faith, to acknowledge, "I am here because my heavenly Father has placed this yoke upon me."

Since Job's life had been greatly blessed, his relationship with the Lord may have been a bit lopsided in understanding tragedy. Did he assume the Lord's blessings were a direct result of him pleasing God, and, therefore, the tragedy that befell him was inexplicable and sent mixed signals regarding God? How often do I presume the same? "I have ease and comfort because I am good and that means I'm earning God's favor." Yet I know from Scripture that David, a man after God's heart, suffered greatly from the unearned hate of his enemies.

How do I justify David's calamity from the hand of, not only his enemies, but also God's enemies? I can't. My finite mind cannot begin to understand the vastness and purposes of God. I see only today. I live in this moment (except in my fears regarding tomorrow). Yet God knew me before I was formed in the womb. His knowledge of me is from the end to before the beginning. He had a plan before my birth. His plans are seldom void of the tragedies of life. He spared not His own life to redeem me unto Himself. So, His love is perfect toward me. I can therefore believe "all" things are somehow for my good...or will become good in my life.

As iron is processed thru heat, cooling, and pressure, I am perfected thru my trials as well as thru my blessings. I am taught to walk by faith, not by sight. Such faith elevates God to His rightful place in my heart; anything less is insulting to Him. When I allow God to operate outside my understanding, I experience Him on a higher level. My flesh screams, "Wait a minute! What about the promise of His Word that says whatsoever I ask Him to do, He will do it?" I remind myself of the list of the faithful who received not their promises in their earthly lives. Did they deserve to suffer more than others? No, in fact, the Scripture says that the world was not worthy of them. It appears they were people the Lord could

Suffering With Purpose

trust to suffer. Their faith, patience, and endurance in suffering make them trophies of honor to the Lord. He can point to each and say, "Their love failed not; their faith stumbled not. Their lives say more about me than all those who have reaped blessings abundantly. These are my chosen ones who have gone to the grave with steadfast faith in spite of their circumstances."

So where does all this leave me? With mixed emotions! Do I want healed to prove my faith, or do I want to prove my faith by allowing God to have His way in my life? My flesh wants to be healed; my heart desires to please the Lord come what may. My flesh maneuvers to escape suffering; my heart yearns to make the Lord proud of me. The degree of my daily suffering causes me to teeter back and forth on which I most desire.

At day's end, I seek rest, but peace is not the absence of adversities. It is identifying with the all-knowing God and allowing Him the reins of my heart, willingly laying down my life at His feet. Peace is not the absence of tribulation but quitting the angst to understand "why" and know He is working all things out for my eternal good. My eternal good is not necessarily my earthly good. Earthly suffering may shape me into the person the Lord will be pleased to marry on the other side. But isn't just making it to heaven enough? I'll take less suffering and squeeze into heaven by the skin of my teeth. Immature thinking at best! Temporal suffering cannot begin to compare with eternal rewards. If I better understood this, I would be more willing to suffer. That brings me back to faith. Mature faith says, "Christ knows best. I will let Him choose what is best for me."

Mature faith! Am I there? Not yet. I wrestle daily with my will versus His will. My will seeks an end from my constant pain and a myriad of dietary restrictions. My will wants all the promises of the

Word now, if not sooner. I don't want a crown of thorns or a halo. I just want to be healed and the sooner the better.

This journey in suffering has raised my awareness of personal weaknesses and insufficiencies. Like a mirror it reflects the real image. I have wrestled with doubts and fears and disbelief. I have pleaded my cause diligently regardless of God's will. I have cried. I have demanded. I have pouted. Some days I have fought back my fears and crossed the bridge to "Not my will, but thine be done." Other days, like Jonah, I have run as far and as fast as I can from God's will.

I'm still confused as to why all the pain and why so long. As for the future for my life on this orb we call earth, I haven't a clue. Strangely, my suffering has helped me come to grips with God's desire to be loved with all my heart, soul, mind, and strength even though I don't understand my circumstances. I really do want to do just that. Am I willing to suffer a bit to attain that goal? I hope so. I want to be able to say with Paul, "For which cause we faint not; but though our outward man perish, yet the inward man is renewed day by day. For our light affliction, which is but a moment, worketh for us a far more exceeding and eternal weight of glory; While we look not at the things which are seen, but at the things which are not seen: for the things which are seen are temporal; but the things which are not seen are eternal" (II Corinthians 4:16-18). To arrive at that conclusion must be worth some pain.[2]

Nancy's journey with pain and uncertainties continues. We're hoping the worst is behind us; we know the best is with us: Jesus. "...I am with you always, even unto the end of the world..." (Matthew 28:20).

Points of Discussion

Discuss why we should not blame God even though He allows suffering. What are disciplines that help us to not blame God?

Why does God allow suffering?

Discuss the concept of mature faith. Is this possible in humans? Do you have it? How can you acquire it?

How may pain refine our love for God?

Chapter 15

Finding Your Rainbow

> Fear thou not; for I am with thee: be not dismayed; for I am thy God: I will strengthen thee; yea, I will help thee; yea, I will uphold thee with the right hand of my righteousness.
>
> Isaiah 41:10

The following testimony was very difficult for my friends in Virginia to write. After much consideration they felt the story would be beneficial to others who had experienced similar loss. The story is that of an entire family; it is written from the perspective of the grandmother.

> My name is Cheryl Williams. My husband, Rex, and I felt God leading us to start a church in historic Farmville, Virginia. We prayed and fasted for sixteen months to be sure we knew God's will. During those months, we made five trips to Farmville and received the approval of our organization to start a church. We moved to Farmville with our three children and within a few months purchased a home in which we held church services. Our first service was March 1987. God blessed our efforts, and we were able to establish a church. We're in our fourth building program. We feel tremendously blessed to have our

three children here serving God with us. We have ten grandchildren, which we love dearly.

Those were some of our victories; now I will tell you the account of the storm of suffering we have endured. May 9, 2009, was a beautiful Saturday and a perfect day for our grandkids to play outside. Our three granddaughters had spent the night. The next day our daughter Kimberly brought her two sons, Lakkun and Addison, along with Skkyler, my oldest daughter's son.

Papaw rode Addison through the woods on the four-wheeler for about an hour. That was a favorite thing Addison enjoyed with Papaw. When they returned, Kim realized Addison needed a diaper change, and being out of diapers, left him with us while she went to get diapers.

The grandkids were getting hungry; so, I decided to go to McDonald's and get Happy Meals. The two older boys were enjoying a computer game. When I went to my car, I noticed the girls and Addison playing way back toward the church. I left, assuming all was well. When I started back from McDonald's, I called my husband. I can't remember why I called him, but I remember he sounded strange and hung up the phone. I had no idea what was wrong. When I arrived home I was surprised to see people everywhere: ambulances, paramedics, police cars. I stopped my Durango in the road several feet before our driveway, wondering what was going on. Kim ran to me sobbing and screaming, "Mom, when you left you ran over Addison, and he's dead. He's dead, Mom. He's not coming back. I've prayed and prayed, but he won't come back."

Words can't describe the horror, the pain, and the shock. My husband stood on our deck, the pain obvious. He saw Addison running toward my Durango just before I pulled out into the road. He tried to get to him in time but could not; so, he saw

Suffering With Purpose

the accident, picked Addison up, and cradled him in his arms as he called 911.

I recall desperately praying, "God, help us to keep a sound mind," because I knew that, without God's help, a tragedy this great could cause us to lose our mind. For the next few days, I tried to stay busy and be strong for my daughter, her husband, my husband, and the rest of the family. I only cried when I was alone because I felt my emotional expressions made it harder for everyone. I grieved deeply, but tried not to break down in front of the family. I knew there must be a time of grieving before healing can come. I needed help with this process; so, I read books on grieving and found there are stages of grief. It seems each person is unique and situations are diverse, but the stages of grieving are similar for all. One particular stage of grief is being angry with God and with others, accusing and blaming. There are certain ways to deal with each stage of grief. If you're reading this story, and you are in a storm from a loss of a loved one, I encourage you to pray, read God's Word, and be open to the support of family and friends. Don't build a wall and seclude yourself from those who love you.

The day after the accident was Sunday, Mother's Day. Though still in shock and feeling tremendous grief, we attended church. My husband and I never stopped worshipping God. Our faith stood firm. If I had not fought for and received personal emotional healing, I believe I would not have been able to love the rest of my grandchildren. In retrospect, if I had built an emotional wall around my life, not wanting to love deeply again because I didn't want to be hurt, I would have missed so much of the joys of life that have come my way after this horrible tragedy.

Our family had many questions, and some felt angry for a time, but we survived what could have destroyed our family. I believe this is due to the prayers of many, our faith in God, and our foundation on His Word. This was not without much effort. A few days after the accident, as I tried to understand, I kept asking, "How could such a tragic thing happen?" God spoke to me about the temporal and the eternal, and He reminded me of a Scripture: "While we look not at the things which are seen, but at the things which are not seen: for the things which are seen are temporal; but the things which are not seen are eternal" (II Corinthians 4:18). This Scripture brought comfort to me. I printed the verse in several different versions and gave a copy to my husband, and it ministered to him also. A few days later a neighboring evangelist took him out for lunch and said to him, "God told me to tell you to not look on what you can see that is temporal but look on what you can't see that's eternal." Wow! God was definitely speaking to us. He knew right where we were and sent someone to let us know.

After the horrific Biblical ordeal of the flood, God gave an encouraging phenomenon to Noah by creating a rainbow. In the first few weeks of our grief, God used the rainbow to comfort us. The day of Addison's funeral a friend gave us a poem about a rainbow. At the service my daughter Allison sang the song "Somewhere Over The Rainbow". A few days after the funeral, Kim and her husband, Chris, and my daughter-in-law Dawn saw a rainbow in the sky. It seemed that God kept encouraging us by this visual that He was watching over us. A few days after that, on Sunday of Memorial Day weekend, our entire family was together at an outdoor church service and cookout; so, I prayed that God would let us see another rainbow while we were all together. I didn't tell anyone else; I just kept praying, "God, send us a rainbow today." During the worship service, as people were praying for Kim and Chris, Dawn said, "Look, there's a rainbow." Needless to say, I got

Suffering With Purpose

so excited, and I told our evangelist's wife, "I was praying for God to send us a rainbow today." She said, "Isn't that neat? And it's upside down, like it's smiling."

Allison researched the upside down rainbow and found: Upside down rainbows are rarely noticed because they are so far overhead. They are formed from refraction of sunlight through ice crystals. Unlike the normal rainbow, they are visible on a very clear day, not a cloudy day. They are only visible for approximately a ten-mile radius. The upside down rainbow God sent us defied the norm. This was a cloudy day. We don't live in a cold climate. We knew God sent that rainbow to that particular ten-mile radius just for us, to remind us that Addison is in heaven with Him, and God is mindful of our loss and pain. Keeping our focus on heaven, and knowing we will see Addison again, has helped our hearts to heal.

The precious memories we have of Addison have helped in our healing. We are thankful to have so many wonderful pictures and some videos. We thank God for the two and one-half years we had him, and we reflect on all the joy he brought. He was so loving and full of life. Anyone could tell by the pictures and videos that he was loved and that he had a happy life. I tell my husband, "Baby, he knew how much you loved him. That's what that day was about, spending time with the grandkids."

I'm also thankful our family stayed close. No one pointed accusing fingers at another. No one yelled angry words. Blaming does no good. We helped each other through this storm.

I was the one that ran over Addison. I realized I couldn't allow the devil, or my self-condemnation, to drive me crazy with the what-ifs. So, I had to think through and sort out in my mind the reasons not to blame myself. In reflection, when I stopped at the end of the drive, I stopped and reread my McDonald's list.

As I sat there Addison ran in front of the vehicle. I couldn't see him because of the height of the Durango and his small stature. After I mentally recreated the scenario, I decided it best that I not continue to replay this scene and dwell on what I could have done differently. I chose to remember Addison's life and the love and joy he brought to us.

It has been hard to write about that horrible day. I am hoping to help someone that is in his or her storm right now. I want to tell you with God's Word to comfort, His help to strengthen, and supportive family and friends, you can make it. It takes time, but you will heal. Make up your mind not to dwell on the negative thoughts, but think on good things.

My husband has had a very hard time because the scene is forever etched in his mind. He had nightmares every night for a long time and still does occasionally. If it had not been for God's love and mercy, we could not have made it. I remember many nights lying awake and praying for my husband until I knew he was asleep. Still, many times he would wake up with a jerk because of the nightmare. I know that our enemy, the devil, would love to use this tragedy to destroy the closeness of our family and to destroy our ministry, but God has not allowed it. Our family has stayed together. We have held onto our faith in God. We have not wavered in serving Him. We are so grateful that individuals have found God because of the testimony of faithfulness during this time of terrible adversity. It has made many realize the God we serve is worth loving and serving, especially in the times of great loss.[1]

Points of Discussion

Discuss how you maintain your faith in God's calling in spite of disaster that befalls you while obeying God's call.

What are the dangers of living with self-blame? How do you avoid blaming yourself?

Discuss the importance of loving again instead of building walls and refusing deep relationships in an attempt to avoid future pain.

How do we cope with significant days (Mother's Day, anniversaries, birthdays, Christmas) that remind us of our loss?

Chapter 16

Christ's Suffering

> Forasmuch then as Christ hath suffered for us in the flesh, arm yourselves likewise with the same mind: for he that hath suffered in the flesh hath ceased from sin;
>
> I Peter 4:1

The subject regarding suffering would be incomplete without reflecting upon the suffering of our Lord: suffering brought about by the sins of mankind, yours and mine included. "Yet it pleased the Lord to bruise Him..." (Isaiah 53:10). Isaiah, prophetically viewing the crucifixion, penned this verse some seven hundred years before it happened. Moreover, God viewed the crucifixion before the creation. In God's omniscience, He perceived man's fall before He created him; consequently, God planned redemption before He created man. The Apostle John described Christ as "...the Lamb slain from the foundation of the world" (Revelation 13:8).

God was the first to suffer. In the space before time, before suffering was a known occasion, God mentally felt disappointment, grief, pain, and rejection. God suffered from His foreknowledge of mankind's failure and rejection of Him. Throughout history God has been scorned by mankind's blatant rebellion. His ultimate suffering came in the Incarnation when at Calvary Christ writhed in ultimate physical and emotional anguish to pay the supreme sacrifice for mankind's redemption: "...the church of God, which he hath purchased with his own blood" (Acts 20:28).

The sin of Adam and Eve brought suffering to all their descendants. Satan was the culprit in the first deception and continues to create havoc among us. His prideful and futile rebellion against God sent him spiraling through the cosmos, on a collision course with destiny. Though Satan is destined for eternal damnation, he presently continues an ongoing attack against God's special creation: mankind.

> And the LORD God said unto the serpent, Because thou hast done this, thou art cursed above all cattle, and above every beast of the field; upon thy belly shalt thou go, and dust shalt thou eat all the days of thy life: And I will put enmity between thee and the woman, and between thy seed and her seed; it shall bruise thy head, and thou shalt bruise his heel. Unto the woman he said, I will greatly multiply thy sorrow and thy conception; in sorrow thou shalt bring forth children; and thy desire shall be to thy husband, and he shall rule over thee. And unto Adam he said, Because thou hast hearkened unto the voice of thy wife, and hast eaten of the tree, of which I commanded thee, saying, Thou shalt not eat of it: cursed is the ground for thy sake; in sorrow shalt thou eat of it all the days of thy life; Thorns also and thistles shall it bring forth to thee; and thou shalt eat the herb of the field; In the sweat of thy face shalt thou eat bread, till thou return unto the ground; for out of it wast thou taken: for dust thou art, and unto dust shalt thou return.
>
> Genesis 3:14-19

Man's expulsion from the garden introduced suffering to all mankind. The curse affected man, the animal kingdom, and all of planet earth. It began the war of millenniums between humanity and Satan. Satan (in the form of a serpent) gained dominion over mankind, ever nipping and wounding his heels, inserting the poisonous venom of sin. When God pronounced the curse for sin, He also articulated Satan's doom. "And I will put enmity between thee and the woman, and between thy seed and her seed; it shall bruise thy head, and thou shalt bruise his heel" (Genesis 3:15). Satan's fate is sealed: his demise assured by Calvary's sacrifice. "And the devil that deceived them was cast into the lake of fire and brimstone, where the beast and the false prophet are, and shall be tormented day and night for ever and ever" (Revelation 20:10).

The result of sin was death: physically and spiritually. Man's redemption necessitated suffering sufficient to satisfy the debt incurred by sin. God chose to defeat Satan, conquer death, and reverse the curse through the Incarnation: God became man and paid, by His death at Calvary, mankind's debt of sin.

> Yet it pleased the LORD to bruise him; he hath put him to grief: when thou shalt make his soul an offering for sin, he shall see his seed, he shall prolong his days, and the pleasure of the LORD shall prosper in his hand. He shall see of the travail of his soul, and shall be satisfied: by his knowledge shall my righteous servant justify many; for he shall bear their iniquities.
>
> Isaiah 53:10-11

Calvary—with its nails, thorns, stripes, shame, and appalling pain—wasn't an afterthought of God. It wasn't a desperate attempt by Him to hopefully wrestle back from Satan a lost creation. A creation with the power of choice had risks, yet God envisioned the end result. He planned Calvary before the creation. Philip Yancey is quoted in multiple sources with this observation:

> "Calvary was a plan of unfathomable love that sanctioned the creation of mankind, for in God's foreknowledge He knew mankind would sin. To have continued the creation with such foreknowledge would seem unimaginable for a loving God, but God determined Calvary as the focal point of all history. Calvary enabled a fallen mankind to enter again into God's holy presence."[1]

The New Testament author of Hebrews described the Incarnation and Calvary:

> Forasmuch then as the children are partakers of flesh and blood, he also himself likewise took part of the same; that through death he might destroy him that had the power of death, that is, the devil; And deliver them who through fear of death were all their lifetime subject to bondage. For verily he took not on him the nature of angels; but he took on him the seed of Abraham. Wherefore in all things it behoved him to be made like unto his brethren, that the might be a merciful and faithful high priest in things pertaining to God, to make reconciliation for the sins of the people. For in that he himself hath suffered being tempted, he is able to succor them that are tempted.
>
> Hebrews 2:14-18

Isaiah, like no other Old Testament prophet, envisioned the Messiah. Ironically, he didn't visualize the Messiah as a conquering warrior, casting off the Roman oppression. He viewed a lamb to the slaughter. Through teary eyes he penned the words:

> He is despised and rejected of men; a man of sorrows, and acquainted with grief: and we hid as it were our faces from him; he was despised, and we esteemed him not. Surely he hath borne our griefs, and carried our sorrows: yet we did esteem him stricken, smitten of God, and afflicted. But he was wounded for our transgressions, he was bruised for our iniquities: the chastisement of our peace was upon him; and with his stripes we are healed. All we like sheep have gone astray; we have turned every one to his own way; and the LORD hath laid on him the iniquity of us all. He was oppressed, and he was afflicted, yet he opened not his mouth: he is brought as a lamb to the slaughter, and as a sheep before her shearers is dumb, so he openeth not his mouth. He was taken from prison and from judgment: and who shall declare his generation? for he was cut off out of the land of the living: for the transgression of my people was he

stricken. And he made his grave with the wicked, and with the rich in his death; because he had done no violence, neither was any deceit in his mouth.

Isaiah 53:3-9

Did you notice the words associated with suffering? Take another look. I count at least twenty in the seven verses: despised, rejected, sorrows, grief, smitten, wounded, bruised, chastisement, stripes, oppressed, afflicted, prison, judgment, stricken, grave, and death. Christ indeed understands our suffering. The crucifixion story, though old and sad, is never out of date. Nor is it out of touch. Consider Calvary from the viewpoint of one who was there that day long ago and who later wrote a letter to the church regarding suffering:

> My name is Simon Peter.
> I'm sure you've heard of me. I was one of the twelve. Along with James and John, Christ chose me to be in His inner circle. Christ placed in my hand the keys to the kingdom of Heaven. On the Day of Pentecost, when the church was born, I was the mouthpiece for God. However, these are my victories. With this writing I share my failures and testify to you of the mighty grace of God in my life. More so, in order for you to relate to Christ during your personal suffering, I want you to visualize the suffering of our Lord.
> Unfortunately, when Christ needed me most, I wasn't there. When Jesus needed someone to speak on His behalf, I denied three times I even knew Him. When He needed someone by His side to bear Him up, I followed afar off.
> I followed afar off as the soldiers roughly escorted Christ from Pilate's Judgment Hall, to Herod's Palace, and back again to Pilate. I stood afar off as Pilate asked the blood-thirsty crowd, "Whom shall I release unto you: Jesus, which is called Christ, or Barabbas?"

"Give us Barabbas."

"Then what shall I do with Jesus?"

"Let Him be crucified!" The frenzied mob thrust their fists into the air.

"Shall I crucify your king?"

"We have no king but Caesar." With those words they released our Lord to be executed.

Pilate washed his hands while the soldiers led away Jesus and two other prisoners.

Anger boiled within me; fear overwhelmed me.

Pushing my way through the crowd, I drew nearer to Jesus. Once alongside the procession, I could see clearly.

A crown of thorns pressed His brow.

They beat Him and yanked out His beard.

Jesus fell. I yearned to run to Him, to lift Him up, to somehow help Him. But, I did not. Another, a stranger, was compelled to carry His cross.

As Jesus struggled to get up, He turned, and for an instant, our eyes met. I reached out to Him, but the crowd separated us. The mob continued down the narrow street. I followed a safe distance from the mob.

At Calvary the procession halted; simultaneously, the crucifixion began. Soldiers pushed the crowd back, grabbed the three condemned, and roughly flung them backward onto the rough, wooden crosses.

Two resisted wildly: screaming, cursing, biting, and kicking. The soldiers harshly subdued them. Jesus didn't resist as they stretched out His arms on the crossbeam. An eerie silence fell upon the bloodthirsty mob. The hammer blows echoed across the Jerusalem valley.

The scene was horrifying. Jesus' muscles jerked as the hardened executioner drove the spikes, first into His hands and then into His feet. The soldiers raised the cross skyward, steadied it for a moment, then dropped it into the prepared hole.

Suffering With Purpose

His flesh tore.

His blood gushed.

He gasped in terror at His pain.

This indescribable pain seemed unbearable for only a few moments, but His agony had only begun. Death by crucifixion was a slow process, planned as such, and it would last all day.

The crowd, like vultures waiting for the death of their prey, huddled in small groups talking among themselves. Trying to justify their merciless actions, one cried out, "You that can destroy the temple and build it again in three days, why don't you save yourself?" Another joined in, "If you are the Son of God, come on down from the cross, and then we will believe." Others nodded their heads and verbalized agreement.

The religious leaders triumphantly joined in, spewing their theological justification. "He saved others, but Himself He can't save. If He be the Christ, as He says He is, let Him come down from the cross. Then we will believe!"

And one of the condemned, through gritted teeth, derided, "If thou be the Christ, save thyself and us." And then he cursed.

Jesus, like a lamb dumb before His shearers, opened not His mouth.

"Why are they treating Him so? What wrong has He done?" There seemed no logical answers for my questions.

The sun rose higher and grew hotter. Time oozed by slowly, like the blood that dripped from the cross, forming a crimson stain on the rocks beneath. I wanted to be near Him, but I remained afar off.

Jesus gritted against the excruciating pain and slowly opened His eyes. Through the blur of blood and tears, it seemed He strained to make out the faces of those present.

I turned my head. I didn't want Him to recognize me, standing among the crowd as if a spectator. He must be terribly disappointed in me.

His lips moved. He struggled to speak. It was a prayer. Though I couldn't make out the words, for I was too great a distance from Him, someone later told me.

"Father, forgive them, for they know not what they do."

Forgive who? The crowd? Those making fun of Him? The soldiers? Those that condemned Him? The self-righteous, religious leaders? Surely not them? And me? Was He praying on my behalf? Somehow I knew He was. He was forgiving all of us. In the mind of Christ, He looked back to the Garden of Eden, and He looked ahead in time, and He suffered for all mankind's sins.

The sky grew black. The sun hid its face from the horrifying scene. The earth shook in huge sobs. Lightning flashed and a cloud burst, washing the tears from the face of His mother. I wished somehow I could comfort her, but any suggestion of comfort would be hypocritical, for I had denied her son.

Again He prayed. This time it was loud and sounded almost triumphant. "It is finished!"

And then He died. All grew silent. It was such a strange feeling. I should have been the one to die. Yet, I was alive. He should have lived. Yet, He was dead. But if He had lived, you and I would remain dead in trespasses and sins.

Staggering through the streets of Jerusalem, I found my way to the upper room where we were staying, where we had eaten the Passover with Him only yesterday. Little did we understand then that He was to become our Passover Lamb.

I had followed Christ afar off. I know now the consequences of doing so. Many times we fail Him out of weakness rather than wickedness. Our vision of His face is unclear. We cannot tell if He is frowning or if He is pleased. Standing afar off we can't quite make out the words He's saying. And there're always others nearer to Him getting His attention. He's touching them, healing them, blessing them. When we serve Christ from a distance, the crowd we end up with doesn't always love the Lord. I wish I'd followed closer.

Early Sunday morning, the women went to His tomb, but they found the stone rolled away and the tomb empty. An angel appeared unto them saying, "Ye seek Jesus of Nazareth, which was crucified. He is not here. He is risen. Go your way, tell His disciples and Peter to meet me in Galilee. Jesus had seen me at Calvary! He saw me standing afar off, but He looked deeper than my faults; He saw my need of salvation. Tell My disciples and Peter! He hadn't abandoned me though I proved weak and cowardly. He was inviting me to meet Him in Galilee. That is where I first met Him. And He met me there again.

When Peter wrote to the suffering Christians, he knew firsthand about suffering. He observed the suffering of our Lord, and he recognized the value of Christ's suffering. He viewed Christ's suffering as purposeful: for mankind's salvation, as proof that all mankind (including Christians) will suffer, as exemplary for future sufferers, as a guarantee of Christ's aid in our suffering.

> For even hereunto were ye called, because Christ also suffered for us, leaving us an example, that ye should follow his steps: Who did no sin, neither was guile found in his mouth: Who, when he was reviled, reviled not again; when he suffered, he threatened not; but committed himself to him that judgeth righteously: Who his own self bare our sins in his own body on the tree, that we, being dead to sins, should live unto righteousness: by whose stripes ye were healed. For ye were as sheep going astray; but

are now returned unto the Shepherd and Bishop of your souls.
I Peter 2:21-25

But and if ye suffer for righteousness' sake, happy are ye: and be not afraid of their terror, neither be troubled; For it is better, if the will of God be so, that ye suffer for well doing, than for evil doing. For Christ also hath once suffered for sins, the just for the unjust, that he might bring us to God, being put to death in the flesh, but quickened by the Spirit:
I Peter 3:14, 17-18

Beloved, think it not strange concerning the fiery trial which is to try you, as though some strange thing happened unto you: But rejoice, inasmuch as ye are partakers of Christ's sufferings; that, when his glory shall be revealed, ye may be glad also with exceeding joy. If ye be reproached for the name of Christ, happy are ye; for the spirit of glory and of God resteth upon you: on their part he is evil spoken of, but on your part he is glorified. But let none of you suffer as a murderer, or as a thief, or as an evildoer, or as a busybody in other men's matters. Yet if any man suffer as a Christian, let him not be ashamed; but let him glorify God on this behalf. Wherefore let them that suffer according to the will of God commit the keeping of their souls to him in well doing, as unto a faithful Creator.
I Peter 4:12-16, 19

Suffering doesn't have to be wasted in our lives. There can be purpose. The apostle presented suffering as having purpose:

The elders which are among you I exhort, who am also an elder, and a witness of the sufferings of Christ, and also a partaker of the glory that shall be revealed: Humble yourselves therefore under the mighty hand of God, that he may exalt you in due time: Casting all your care upon him; for he careth for you. Be sober, be vigilant; because your adversary the devil, as a roaring lion, walketh about, seeking whom he may devour: Whom resist stedfast in the faith, knowing that the same afflictions are accomplished in your brethren that are in the world. But the God of all grace, who hath called us unto his eternal glory by Christ Jesus, after that ye have suffered a while, make you perfect, stablish, strengthen, settle you.

I Peter 5:1, 6-10

We can take courage in our suffering, for our Lord, likewise, suffered and is full of compassion toward us. He sees us in our suffering, He feels our pain, and He understands. Though possessing the power to change the circumstances, He may choose to walk with us in our suffering, exposing us to pain, but extending to us sufficient grace to accomplish His will.

It is difficult to see immediate value in suffering; indeed, like Job, we may never understand why, but there is eternal value, though we may not understand unless revealed by the Holy Spirit.

The Apostle Paul suffered much for the gospel. Had he continued to reject Christianity, he probably would have become one of the more noted Jewish scholars and leaders, but he walked away from an exceptional religious future by accepting Christianity. Through much persecution Paul acquired a unique grasp on the subject of suffering. He felt it insufficient to know Christ only in the power of the resurrection (receiving only the blessings of the Lord), but he also wanted to know Christ in "the fellowship of His sufferings" (Philippians 3:10). The resurrection was the celebration of victory. Paul didn't want only to celebrate; He wanted to experience the battle: to be a part of the fight. The battle was the garden of agony, the crown of thorns, the jeering crowds, the broken and bruised body, the nails, the cross, and the gasps for another breath. Paul asks, how can we celebrate alongside Christ, but refuse to suffer for Him and with Him? Is the servant greater or even equal to his lord? Of course we know we aren't greater or equal to Christ, yet He suffered. "If we suffer" (endure or persevere), Paul wrote to Timothy, whom

Paul was encouraging to remain strong in grace even in the midst of hardship, "we shall also reign with Him" (II Timothy 2:12). He further challenged the concept of Christianity without suffering. "Every man's work shall be made manifest: for the day shall declare it, because it shall be revealed by fire; and the fire shall try every man's work of what sort it is" (I Corinthians 3:13).

I hope you are beginning to see the eternal value of your sufferings. But have we learned to cope better? Does the pain become less with each generation? Have we gained insight from the past to desensitize the hurt of the present? I dare say, "No". We may respond differently, depending upon the many variables, but the hurt is basically the same. Pain is pain. The suffering goes on. From Genesis to Revelation, suffering is evident in every drama, and the sequels seem endless. But it will end! For God has promised to personally bring an end to suffering. To this promise we must cling.

> And I saw a new heaven and a new earth: for the first heaven and the first earth were passed away; and there was no more sea. And I John saw the holy city, new Jerusalem, coming down from God out of heaven, prepared as a bride adorned for her husband. And I heard a great voice out of heaven saying, Behold, the tabernacle of God is with men, and he will dwell with them, and they shall be his people, and God himself shall be with them, and be their God. And God shall wipe away all tears from their eyes; and there shall be no more death, neither sorrow, nor crying, neither shall there be any more pain: for the former things are passed away. And he that sat upon the throne said, Behold, I make all things new. And he said unto me, Write: for these words are true and faithful. And he said unto me, It is done. I am Alpha and Omega, the beginning and the end. I will give unto him that is athirst of the fountain of the water of life freely. He that overcometh shall inherit all things; and I will be his God, and he shall be my son.
>
> Rev. 21:1-7

Suffering With Purpose

These are the "be no more" promises of God. Some day there will be no more tears, death, sorrow, crying, and pain. "But, I want to feel better now!" we respond. Nevertheless, we must replace feelings with faith: faith in God and faith in His promises to us recorded in the Bible. "Henceforth there is laid up for me a crown of righteousness, which the Lord, the righteous judge, shall give me at that day: and not to me only, but unto all them also that love his appearing" (II Timothy 4:8).

What about your suffering? Perhaps it doesn't make any sense. Surely there can be no good coming from your pain. Do you feel your suffering is meaningless? I encourage you to look closer, not at the suffering; look at the possibilities. Consider your suffering as God's opportunity to bring greater purpose into your life. Learn from the study of Job's suffering. Take courage in Christ's example of suffering. With the proper mental attitude, your suffering will transform you from the earthly-minded, temporal thinker into a celestial-bound, eternally-focused person of purpose. "And be not conformed to this world: but be ye transformed by the renewing of your mind, that ye may prove what is that good, and acceptable, and perfect, will of God" (Romans 12:2). We are familiar with the term metamorphosis when considering the biological process of something being changed after its natural birth or hatching process. The process is somewhat dreadful; the result is splendidness. The root Greek word was translated into the King James Bible as being changed or transformed, and the concept is used in the process of our being changed from what we are biologically to what God wants us to become. There are various resources God uses to transform us, one of them being suffering. We dare not allow suffering, which can make us more like Christ, to cause us to become cynical, angry, and full of bitterness.

What about you? Where are you in the process? Are those battle scars on your body? Do I sense weariness in your stride? Don't you dare throw in the towel; Christ is watching, and angels are ringsiders, awaiting His command. From heaven's perspective all is well. Your fight isn't an isolated engagement; it fits into a much bigger picture. There's a purpose only eternity may reveal.

I hear the echo of words millenniums past, "...Have you noticed my friend Job? There's no one quite like him—honest and true to his word, totally devoted to God and hating evil" (Job 1:8).[2] The circumstances are similar, but the name of the servant has changed. Your trial is evidence of God's presence; evidently, He believes in you.

Paul described our vision this side of heaven, which is blurry at best, when he said, "For now we see through a glass, darkly…" (I Corinthians 13:12). Heaven's perspective reveals a clearer image regarding suffering. Could that be a golden crown forming in the fiery furnace of your suffering? Are those nail-scared hands tempering the crown to fit your head? Is that an angelic choir stage right? Is that a smile on Christ's face? I believe it is; further, I believe it's for you.

Points of Discussion

Why and how did Christ's suffering please the Lord?

How can God suffer?

How did man's sin in the garden perpetuate suffering?

What is the significance of Christ's suffering?

What value is there in your suffering?

When and how will suffering be eradicated?

Larry M. Arrowood

Special Thanks

A consortium of wonderful people made this book possible. I am indebted to each of them for their support, talents, and commitments to this project.

Thanks to Nancy Arrowood and Tammy Fisher for their many hours of editing. Thanks to friends who relived their pain as they shared their stories, solely motivated by the desire to help someone who is going through similar circumstances. Thanks to Lightning Source for walking us through the process of printing. Thanks to Woodsong Publishers for the opportunity to have another book in print. Thanks to my wonderful church congregation who allows me the time to write. Thanks to Christ for giving inspiration through His Word and by His example.

Endnotes

Chapter 1

[1] Jim Rohn, The Seasons of Life, Jim Rohn International, 1981.
[2] Mark Batterson, The Circle Maker, (Grand Rapids, MI, Zondervan, 2011), 78-79.

Chapter 2

[1] Charles R. Swindoll, Job: A Man of Heroic Endurance, (Nashville, TN, The Word Publishing Group, 2004), 5.

Chapter 4

[1] Eugene H. Peterson, Scripture taken from The Message. Copyright © 1993, 1994, 1995, 1996, 2000, 2001, 2002. Used by permission of NavPress Publishing Group.
[2] Helen Keller, American Author (1880-1968).

Chapter 6

[1] Mayo Clinic staff, Forgiveness, Letting go of grudges and bitterness, (Website: http://www.mayoclinic.com/health/forgiveness/MH00131).
[2] Meir, Minirth, Wichern, Ratcliff, Introduction to Psychology and Counseling, Second Edition, (Grand Rapids, MI., Baker Book House, 1991), 77.
[3] Elizabeth Landau, Anger at God common, even among atheists, (CNN website: www.thechart.blogs.cnn.com/2011/01/01/anger-at-god-common-even-among-atheists/, January 1, 2011).

Chapter 7

[1] John Charles Ryle (1816-1900)
[2] Author and editor Donald C. Stamps, The Full Life Study Bible, 1991, notes for Job 7:11, 770.

[3] Brenda Goodman, Foreginess Is Good, Up to a Point, (Psychology Today website: http://www.psychologytoday.com/articles/200402/forgiveness-is-good-point), January 1, 2004.

Chapter 8

[1] Eugene H. Peterson, Scripture taken from The Message. Copyright © 1993, 1994, 1995, 1996, Job 1:11-3.

Chapter 9

[1] The author's very loose paraphrase of Matthew 25:31-46.

Chapter 10

[1] Email from Mark Cottrill, Burbon, Indiana, 2012.
[2] Told by Rick Schafstall, Seymour, Indiana 2012.

Chapter 11

[1] Submitted by Dennis and Evelyn Croucher, Knoxville, Tennessee, 2012.
[2] Quoted from a sermon by Evangelist Michael Easter, 2012.

Chapter 12

[1] Submitted by Bethany Johnson, Seymour, Indiana, 2012.

Chapter 13

[1] Submitted by Thomas Marek, 2012.

Chapter 14

[1] Paul Ciholas, Consider My Servant Job, (Peabody, MA., Hendrickson Publishers, Inc., 1998), 25.
[2] Submitted by Nancy Arrowood, Seymour, Indiana, 2012

Chapter 15

[1] Submitted by Cheryl Williams, Farmville, Virginia, 2012

Chapter 16

[1] Philip Yancey, American Christian author, (1949).
[2] Eugene H. Peterson, Scripture taken from The Message. Copyright © 1993, 1994, 1995, 1996, Job 1:8.

CPSIA information can be obtained
at www.ICGtesting.com
Printed in the USA
FFOW01n1946280416
23621FF